About this Book

Microcomputers and microcontrollers have found their way into every aspect of our daily lives. Amongst other things, they are responsible for heating our homes, cooking our food, managing the engines in our cars, and controlling our home media.

At first sight microcontrollers can appear to be extremely complex, but unlike many other technologies, experimenting with them is something that you can do at home with limited resources and with a minimal outlay. In addition to a PC, laptop or tablet for developing your code, a soldering iron, a multi-meter, and a handful of components are all that you need. Except, of course, for some ideas to get you started—and that's exactly where this book comes in!

The book will provide you with the basic underpinning knowledge necessary to develop your own code and use it in conjunction with the mictro:bit's built-in sensors and transducers as well as a variety of external devices such as LEDs, buttons, switches, sounders, relays and motors. Each chapter is devoted to a different aspect of the micro:bit and each concludes with a practical project designed to take you further along the road of building and coding your own micro:bit applications.

The book is designed specifically for newcomers and it assumes no previous coding experience. It also makes no assumptions about previous experience of electronic construction. Many of the practical projects can be assembled without soldering and some require no external circuitry whatsoever.

The book is ideal for students and teachers. It is equally well suited to those who may be returning to study or who may be studying independently as well as those who may need a quick refresher.

The book has ten chapters, each dealing with a particular topic, and two appendices. Coding techniques are introduced on a progressive basis and delivered in manageable chunks. In addition, self-test questions can be found at the end of each chapter and solutions are provided at the end of the book.

About the author

Mike Tooley has over 30 years of teaching electronics, electrical principles, computing and avionics to engineers and technicians, previously as Head of Department of Engineering and Vice Principal at Brooklands College in Surrey, UK. He currently works as a consultant and freelance technical author and lives in West Sussex.

Mike is the author many popular engineering textbooks used in Further and Higher Education Colleges and he has also been a long standing contributor to Everyday with Practical Electronics and recently as the author of the popular Teach-In series devoted to the Raspberry Pi, Arduino and BBC micro:bit.

Mike's interest in microcomputers started over 40 years ago, with early 8-bit microprocessors such as the 6800, 6502 and Z80. He is an avid electronic enthusiast and is currently spending his spare time experimenting with software defined radio (SDR). He is an active radio amateur and a holder of British and French amateur call signs.

Contents

6

Decisions 49

7

Digital I/O 59

8

Analogue I/O 73

9

Sensing temperature   85

10

Sensing motion   95

Answers to questions   103

Useful web addresses   106

Index   107

A note to teachers and lecturers

The book is ideal for students following formal courses in schools, sixth-form colleges, and further education colleges. It is equally well suited for use as a text that can support distance or flexible learning and for those who may need a 'hands-on' guide before studying at a higher level.

While the book assumes little previous knowledge, students need to be able to manipulate simple formulae and understand some basic electrical concepts, such as the relationship between the voltage, current and resistance in a simple electrical circuit.

Our 'Going further' projects have been designed to provide learners with 'hands-on' experience. These should be considered open-ended and can be modified or extended to suit the needs of individual learners. The aim should be that of giving students 'food for thought' and encouraging learners to develop their own solutions and interpretation of the topic. Each project introduces various different concepts in coding and electronics. For example, the use of MOSFET switching devices as a means of interfacing external devices is introduced in Chapter 7, while PWM techniques for generating analogue voltages is introduced in Chapter 8.

Assuming a notional delivery time of 1.5 hours per week, the material contained in this book (together with practical projects) will require approximately 12 weeks (one academic term) for delivery. When developing a teaching programme it is, of course, essential to check that you comply with the requirements of the awarding body concerning assessment and syllabus coverage.

A word about safety

When working on electronic circuits, personal safety (both yours and of those around you) should be paramount in everything that you do and, even though the micro:bit operates at low voltage, interface circuits can operate at much higher potential and so it is wise to get into the habit of treating all electronic circuits with great care.

Hazards can exist within many circuits—even those that, on the face of it, may appear to be totally safe. Potential hazards can usually be easily recognized and it is well worth making yourself familiar with them. You should always think carefully before working on circuits where mains or high voltages (i.e. voltages of 50V or more) are present. Failure to observe this simple precaution can result in a very real risk of electric shock.

Bodily contact with mains or high-voltage circuits can be lethal. The most critical path for electric current within the body (i.e. the one that is most likely to stop the heart) is that which exists from one hand to the other. The hand-to-foot path is also dangerous but somewhat less dangerous than the hand-to-hand path.

So, before you start to work on an item of mains-operated equipment, it is essential not only to switch off but to disconnect the equipment at the mains by removing the mains plug. If you have to make measurements or carry out adjustments on an item of working (or 'live') equipment, a useful precaution is that of using one hand only to perform the adjustment or to make the measurement. The other hand should be placed safely away from contact with anything metal.

Getting started

What is the BBC micro:bit?

Originally intended as a learning resource for students in all UK secondary schools, the BBC micro:bit is a tiny programmable circuit board that will let you easily code and develop your own real-world applications. Despite its diminutive footprint, the BBC micro:bit has all of the features of a fully fledged microcontroller together with a simple 5×5 LED matrix display, two buttons, and various sensors including an accelerometer, a magnetometer, and a light sensor. The board can be powered and programmed by means of a USB cable and it has Bluetooth interface for simple wireless applications.

The micro:bit can be programmed in several different ways but, if you are new to coding, the easiest way is to use the

Figure 1.1 The BBC micro:bit

micro:bit's dedicated visual programming environment, known as Microsoft Block Editor. This is a highly intuitive cloud-based application and it will enable you to get your own code up and running in the quickest possible time. All you need to do is select the pre-built blocks of code that you wish to use and then drag and connect them into your own code.

The Microsoft Block Editor will also let you develop and test your code using a 'virtual' micro:bit. When you are happy with the result you can compile your code on-line, download it and flash it to your micro:bit which will appear as a USB drive when connected to your PC, laptop or tablet.

Figure 1.2 Micro:bit coding is easy using the Code Block editor

Getting connected

Before going any further you might like to check out some of the data on your own micro:bit. Just connect it to any vacant USB port on your computer. This will supply 5V DC power to the micro:bit and allow it to communicate with your PC. Once communication has been established your micro:bit will appear as a new drive. If you open the new drive you will see that it contains several files and folders. Click on the file called DETAILS and you will be presented with information that is unique to your own circuit board. At this stage, you don't need to worry too much about the information but at least you will know that your micro:bit is talking to your host computer!

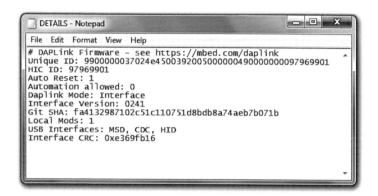

Figure 1.3 BBC micro:bit data can be found in the DETAILS text file

Getting technical

The micro:bit's processor is a tiny 32-bit nRF51822 (ARM Cortex M0) from Nordic Semiconductor. This is a powerful reduced instruction set (RISC) machine designed specifically for energy and space-efficient applications. The processor has 256KB flash memory and 16KB of static RAM. The ARM core has the capability to switch between 16 MHz or 32.768 kHz.

The processor is supported by an NXP/Freescale KL26Z. This 48 MHz device relieves the processor from the burden of communication by providing a full-speed USB 2.0 OTG (on-the-go) interface for external devices. The KL26Z also provides the voltage regulation from the USB supply, converting the nominal 5V USB supply to a nominal 3.3V for the processor and other support devices. This supply is also made available at the edge connector. Some of the key specifications are shown in Table 1.1 below.

Processor	32-bit Nordic Semiconductor nRF51822
Clock speed	16MHz (32.768kHz switchable)
USB controller	NXP/Freescale KL26Z
Memory	256K flash plus 16K static RAM
Wireless	2.4GHz Bluetooth low energy (BLE)
Display	25 red LEDs in a 5×5 matrix
I/O connector	23-pin edge connector (1.27mm pitch)
DC supply	5V nominal (via USB) or 3.3V battery
Dimensions	43mm × 52mm

Table 1.1 BBC micro:bit specifications

On-board sensors and transducers

A variety of useful sensors and interfaces are provided on-board. These include a 3-axis magnetometer and a 3-axis accelerometer as well as light and temperature sensors. For communication and interfacing the board is provided with Universal Serial Bus (USB), universal asynchronous receiver/transmitter (UART), Serial Peripheral Interface (SPI), and Inter-integrated Circuit Interface (I^2C) facilities. The board also has two buttons for user input. These are labelled A and B.

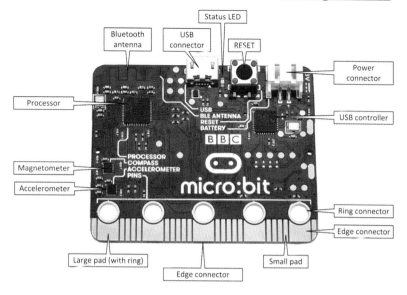

Figure 1.4 BBC micro:bit board layout

The edge connector

The edge connector consists of five large pads with rings interspersed with 20 smaller pads. The five large pads permit connection to the board using crocodile clips and banana plugs. Due to their small size, the remaining pins should only be accessed using an appropriate edge connector. This will also provide access to the large pads with several of the edge connector pins being effectively shorted together by the wider pads.

The five large pads and rings are designed for connection of crocodile clips or 4mm banana plugs. Three of these five pads (labelled 0, 1 and 2) are available for general purpose input and output (GPIO) whilst the two remaining large pads provide access to the 3.3V DC supply and 0V ground (GND). If you intend using the edge connector pads as a supply for external circuitry we recommend that you limit the current demand to a maximum of 50mA (and in no case more than 90mA). Furthermore, take great care when using crocodile clips as they can easily make contact with adjacent pads. An inadvertent short between 3.3V and GND can cause permanent damage!

Pin	Function	Use
0[1]	GPIO	General purpose digital I/O, analogue and PWM
1[1]	GPIO	General purpose digital I/O, analogue and PWM
2[1]	GPIO	General purpose digital I/O, analogue and PWM
3	LED Col. 1	Can be used for GPIO when LED display not used[2]
4	LED Col. 2	Can be used for GPIO when LED display not used[2]
5	Button A	GPIO etc. shared with on-board Button A
6	LED Col. 9	Can be used for GPIO when LED display not used[2]
7	LED Col. 8	Can be used for GPIO when LED display not used[2]
8	GPIO	General purpose digital I/O, analogue and PWM
9	LED Col. 7	Can be used for GPIO when LED display not used[2]
10	LED Col. 3	Can be used for GPIO when LED display not used[2]
11	Button B	GPIO etc. shared with on-board Button A
12	GPIO	GPIO etc.[3]
13	GPIO	GPIO etc. (also SCLK for SPI bus applications)
14	GPIO	GPIO etc. (also MISO for SPI bus applications)
15	GPIO	GPIO etc. (also MOSI for SPI bus applications)
16	GPIO	General purpose digital I/O, analogue and PWM
17	3.3V	3.3V positive supply[4]
18	3.3V	3.3V positive supply[4]
19	I^{2}C SCL	Serial clock for the I^{2}C bus[5]
20	I^{2}C SDA	Serial data available for the I^{2}C bus[5]
21	GND	Ground (common negative supply)[6]
22	GND	Ground (common negative supply)[6]

Table 1.2 Default functions associated with the edge connector pins

Notes:

1. Pins 0, 1 and 2 are large pads with rings.

2. Pins 3, 4, 6, 7, 9 and 10 are associated with the matrix LED display and also with the micro:bit's ambient light sensing mode.

3. Although pin-12 is currently available for general purpose use it should be considered as "reserved for future use". Future versions of the micro:bit may use this pin for a dedicated purpose.

4. Pins 17 and 18 are for the positive supply which is also available from the adjacent large pad labelled '3V'.

5. Pins 19 and 20 are used by the I^2C bus. This bus is used by the on-board accelerometer and magnetometer chips and so care must be taken if you intend to use these pins for any other I/O functions.

6. Pins 21 and 22 are directly linked to the large pad labelled 'GND'. Note that this pad is not numbered.

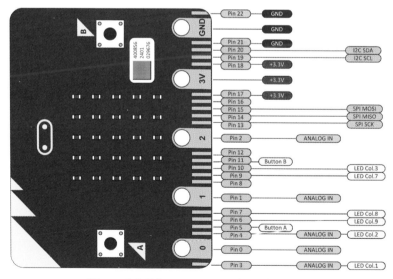

Figure 1.5 Edge connector pin assignment

Using buttons to replicate external inputs

The functions of the two buttons (labelled A and B) are respectively duplicated on pin-5 and pin-11 of the edge connector. This simply means that, if pin-5 is taken low (i.e. connected to GND) it has the same effect as pressing button A. Similarly, if pin-11 is taken low, this will have the same effect as pressing button B. This feature can be quite handy as it will allow you to use a button press to simulate the signal from a switch or external digital sensor without having the device physically present and connected to the micro:bit.

The status LED

The status LED (see Fig. 1.4) will become illuminated whenever the micro:bit is connected to the USB port of a powered host computer. It also flashes when data is being downloaded and transferred into the micro:bit's static memory. The status LED will also be illuminated when the board is being powered from a USB power adapter. When powered from a battery pack there is *no* power indication unless the LED matrix display is being used!

Batteries and holders

When using a battery to supply power to the micro:bit you will need some form of battery holder. Unfortunately, the battery holder supplied with the standard micro:bit kit is not fitted with a switch so it becomes necessary to repeatedly connect and disconnect the power connector. If left connected, the batteries will drain unnecessarily and since this type of power connector is not designed for repeated connection and disconnection it would be wise to incorporate a switch in the supply connection (see Fig. 1.6). Alternatively, battery connectors fitted with switches are available from several suppliers and these can usefully replace those supplied with a basic micro:bit kit.

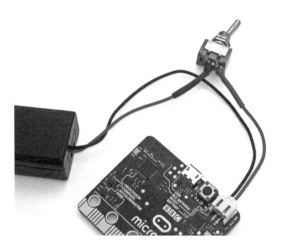

Figure 1.6 Fitting a switch to the battery connector

One neat solution to the need for a battery pack is available from Kitronik (https://www.kitronik.co.uk/). This company has developed their MI:power board (see Fig. 1.7) to fit snugly behind the micro:bit (see Fig. 1.1). The MI:power board is fitted with a 3V "coin cell" holder (CR2032), an on/off switch, and a piezo buzzer. the board is connected directly to the 3V, GND and P0 connections on the micro:bit. The built in buzzer is connected to the P0 pad (the default output pin when using the audio functions in the Microsoft Block Editor software).

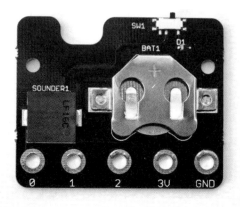

Figure 1.7 The MI:power board

Maximum load

The current drive that can be obtained from any one of the micro:bit's I/O pins should be no more than 5mA. Furthermore, the board is only rated for a total I/O load of 15mA. In addition to limiting the output current for resistive loads you should also avoid connecting loads that are highly reactive (i.e. inductive or capacitive). Loudspeakers, solenoids and motors in particular may generate significant back-EMF whenever current is removed from them and the reverse voltages generated can often exceed the maximum ratings for the GPIO pins. Later we will show you how you can easily get over these restriction with some simple external circuitry. Finally, no more than 75mA should be taken from the micro:bit's 3V pad.

Creating micro:bit applications

The BBC micro:bit was developed as a platform for teaching coding and it supports several quite different programming environments. The most basic of these is the Microsoft Block Editor visual environment. This dispenses completely with text-based coding and uses a simple drag and drop programming environment which is very easy to learn and makes an ideal starting point for anyone with no programming experience.

With the aid of code blocks it is possible to produce a simple application in a matter of minutes and then have the graphical source (basically a picture of what the code will be doing) converted on-line into a hexadecimal file which can be downloaded to your computer and then copied to the micro:bit via the USB connection. This is quite straightforward but it does require a working internet connection to the web-based application via the user's browser.

There are currently four freely accessible development environments available from the micro:bit website (http://www.microbit.org). To get started you just need to click on 'Create code' and choose your preferred programming environment. Next we will summarise their main features.

The Microsoft Block Editor

Microsoft Block Editor is a very simple visual editor with a user-friendly drag and drop interface. The editor is designed to introduce structured programming. If you want to avoid the complexities of a text-based interface this is the one to start with. Later you can convert scripts produced by Microsoft Block Editor into scripts that will work with Microsoft Touch Develop, once again providing a straightforward upgrade path to text-based coding.

Code Kingdom Javascript

Like the Microsoft Block Editor, the Code Kingdom's Javascript editor also provides you with a drag and drop environment in which each of blocks represents a chunk of code. The interface makes it possible to switch easily between the visual environment and a text-based editor. Code Kingdom's Javascript makes the transition to text-based programming relatively straightforward.

Microsoft PXT

Microsoft's Programming Experience Toolkit (PXT) provides a coding environment that supports both a block-based editor and JavaScript. It also provides support for low-power wireless peer-to-peer communication.

Microsoft Touch Develop

Another package from Microsoft, Touch Develop, is intended for use with mobile touchscreen devices (such as tablets and smartphones). The software can also be used with a conventional PC, keyboard and mouse.

Touch Develop can be used to produce platform-independent web-based applications. Unfortunately Touch Develop is not currently compatible with the standard Android browser. If you need to develop your code on an Android platform you will need to change your browser to Google Chrome.

MicroPython

MicroPython uses a text-based editor (there is no graphical programming environment) but this will probably not be a great concern for those with previous coding experience.

There is currently plenty of support for MicroPython from an active community of developers and enthusiasts. The Mu editor (available from www.https://codewith.mu/) can be downloaded and used off-line. This simple and straightforward   text editor is available for Windows, OSX and Linux.

Which one to use?

If you have no previous experience of coding, we recommend that you start with the Microsoft Block Editor. This uses a highly intuitive visual environment and it will give you a taste of coding without having to resort to editing text.

At some later stage, you will probably find the need to move to text-based editing and at that point we would suggest the MicroPython environment as this language is both well supported and available for multiple platforms.

Next, in Chapter 2 we will introduce Microsoft Code Blocks in more detail and help you to create your first BBC micro:bit program. If you already have some experience of using Code Blocks you could move straight on to Chapter 3.

Going further—a virtual micro:bit

You will need a computer with a working internet connection. Open your web browser and use it to visit the BBC micro:bit website (http://www.microbit.org/). Next click on Let's Code and then scroll down to view the different editors that are available from the micro:bit's website.

Locate Microsoft Block Editor and then click on Get started with this editor. This will take you to the Code Block editor—you now have a virtual micro:bit to play with!

Questions

1. How many LEDs are used in the micro:bit's on board display?

2. What type of processor is used in the micro:bit?

3. What DC supply voltage does the micro:bit require?

4. What do the initials 'UART' stand for?

5. How are connections made to the micro:bit?

6. What two interface bus standards are supported by the micro:bit?

Introducing code blocks

What are code blocks?

Code blocks are simply chunks of ready-made code that can be inserted into your own code. Code blocks allow you to quickly and easily produce an application without having to resort to the use of a text-based editor. Each block of reusable code is represented graphically by symbols that behave in a similar way to that of a jigsaw piece, slotting together to form a complete program.

The Microsoft Block Editor environment (see Fig. 2.1) provides a means of assembling code blocks into a complete application. On the left of the editor screen you will find a library of available code blocks sorted into the

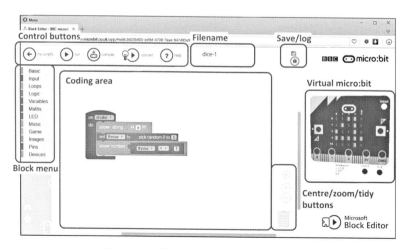

Figure 2.1 The Microsoft Block editor

following categories: Basic, Input, Loops, Logic, Variables, Maths, LED, Music, Games, Images, Pins and Devices.

The centre of the display provides a coding area for you to assemble blocks of code. You simply select the blocks that you need from the library on the left and then drag and drop them into your code. Once there, blocks can be dragged around and linked together in order to produce a complete program. Happily, this couldn't be easier!

On the right of the Microsoft Block Editor screen is a "virtual" micro:bit complete with buttons and LED matrix display. The board can also be tilted and rotated. This excellent feature allows you to test your newly developed program without having to connect and download your code to a real micro:bit. To test your code on a real micro:bit you will first need to connect it to your host computer via the USB cable and micro USB connector. If you have not done this before you may find that your host computer needs to locate a USB driver for your micro:bit.

The process of locating and installing the driver will usually be automatic but you might see a notification that the driver has been located and is being installed. Finally, when you are ready to send your code to the micro:bit you just need to click on the buttons at the top of the screen to generate and download a hexadecimal (.hex) file. When successfully downloaded this file will appear in your downloads folder. When you've located the downloaded .hex file all you need to do is to send or copy it to the USB drive that your operating system has allocated to your micro:bit.

Getting started—a simple button counter

Let's start with something really simple: counting button presses. For this very simple application we will use Button A as an input and display the number of presses that it receives by scrolling the count on the matrix LED display. We will use a variable called count to hold the number of presses and increment it (i.e. add 1 to the value of count) each time Button A is pressed. Note that it is good practice to initialise the value of count by setting it to zero when the program first starts but this will be done automatically when we define the new variable. Finally, in order to restart counting (from 0) we will detect and use Button B to reset the current value of count to zero. Now let's walk through the process of developing and testing the code.

First open Microsoft Block Editor (as described earlier) and enter a name for your program in the text field at the top of the screen. Your source file will be stored under this name and it will also appear in the name of the hexadecimal (.hex) file downloaded to your host computer following on-line compilation of your code.

Next select Basic from the blocks menu on the left and then select the forever block and drag it into the code window. Position it towards the left of the code window. Next return to the block menu and select Basic from the blocks menu for a second time. This time locate show number, select it then drag it into the code window (as shown in Fig. 2.3). Now select Variables from the blocks menu. Locate the item block and then drop it into the editing area (as shown in Fig, 2.3). You will now have three blocks of code ready to be connected together!

2 Introducing code blocks

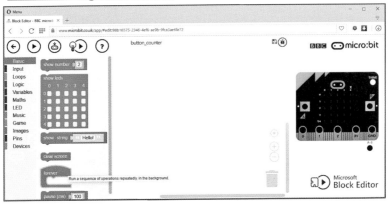

Figure 2.2 Selecting the forever *code block from the Basic library*

The three blocks of code are linked together by simply dragging and dropping (the blocks will join together rather like the pieces of a a jigsaw puzzle). Fig. 2.4 shows how this is done. First drag the item variable and drop it into the grey area inside the show number block. You should find that it easily drops into place, replacing the number. Next you need to drag the entire show number block into the slot

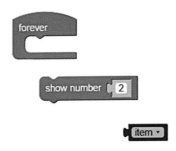

Figure 2.3 The first three block of code dropped in the editing area

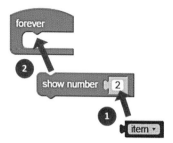

Figure 2.4 The first three block of code dropped in the editing area

in the forever block. Once again, this should easily move and drop into place with the forever block readjusting itself to accommodate the show number block.

Next we need to change the default variable name, item, to something a little more meaningful. We need to tell the code that the number that we want to display is the current value of our variable, count. Click inside the item box and open the pop-up dialogue box Then select New variable and enter count as the new variable name, see Fig. 2.5).

We need two more sections of code. One will check to see if button A is pressed and the other will check to see if button B has been pressed. In the first case we need to increase the value of count (effectively adding one to whatever the value is) and in the second we need to reset the count by changing its value to 0. The required code is shown in Fig. 2.6. You will need to use the Input library for the blocks of code that read the state of the buttons and the Maths library to insert the value 0. You will also need to change item to count by clicking on the down arrow.

2 Introducing code blocks

Figure 2.5 The first three block of code dropped in the editing area

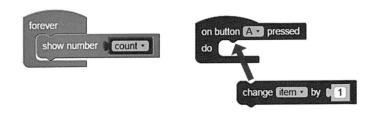

Figure 2.6 Adding code that reacts to the state of button A

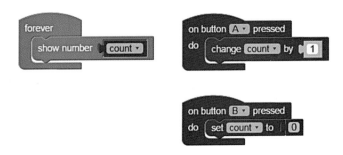

Figure 2.7 The final code ready to test

What does this all do? Let's just look back at what we've just done. The forever block ensures that the program continues in an infinite loop for as long as power is applied to the micro:bit. On button A pressed reacts to a press on button A and increments (i.e. adds 1) to the value of the variable, count. On button B pressed reacts to a press on button B, setting the count back to zero so we can start again. To test the code you just need to click on the run arrow (second from the left). When you do this the display will become illuminated and the number of times button A is pressed will appear on the LED display. Pressing button B will set the count back to 0 (see Fig. 2.8).

When you are ready to test the code for real, connect your micro:bit via USB, press the compile button in the Block Editor, wait for your code to be compiled and downloaded and then copy the hex. file to the USB drive that corresponds to your micro:bit. When the micro:bit resets itself you should now have your very first micro:bit application up and running!

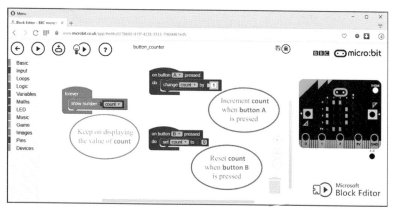

Figure 2.8 The final code ready to test

Going further—micro:bit dice

This first micro:bit project involves the development of a simple dice application. Using the micro:bit's on-board accelerometer it is possible to detect when the board is shaken. To do this you can use the on shake code block. The micro:bit's pick random code block will return a random number within the range specified.

The number returned will range from 0 to whatever upper integer is specified. If we set this upper limit to 5 the routine will generate random numbers from 0 to 5. By adding 1 to whatever number is generated we will have random numbers ranging from 1 to 6, corresponding to the number of faces on a dice. We have used throw as our variable and displayed an initial '*' each time the dice is thrown (or shaken in our case!).

Don't forget to name and save your code before testing it. Finally, we used an MI:power board (see pages 9 and 10) to provide power for the finished unit.

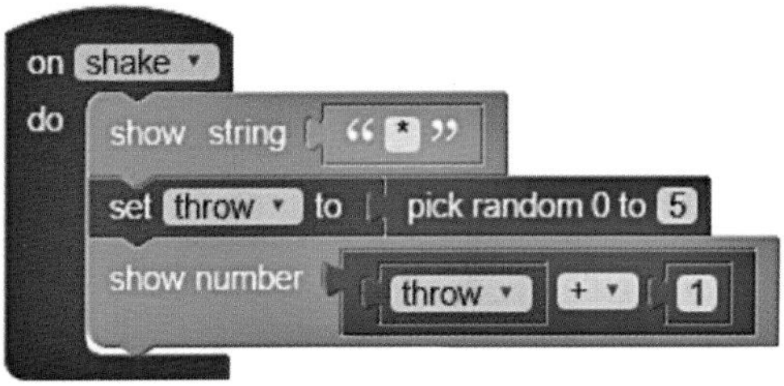

Figure 2.9 The micro:bit dice application

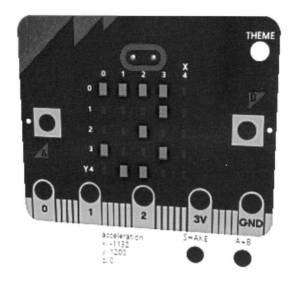

Figure 2.10 The virtual micro:bit dice

Figure 2.11 Complete micro:bit dice (with power board attached)

Questions

1. What type of file is downloaded following successful compilation of a micro:bit application?

2. In which of the Microsoft Block Editor libraries will you find the code that reads the state of buttons A and B?

3. How can the name of a variable be changed from the default value allocated by the Code Editor?

4. When a variable is incremented what happens to its value?

5. What is the purpose of the forever code block?

6. What is the lowest value of random integer number that the micro:bit's pick random code block can generate?

3

Using the LED display

How does the LED display work?

In Chapter 2 we made use of the micro:bit's in-built LED matrix to display the output from our dice application. Despite its obvious simplicity, the LED matrix is quite versatile and will do a lot more than just display numbers. One of the most useful features is the ability to scroll simple text messages. For example, 'Press any button to start', 'Alarm set' or 'Frost warning!'.

The example shown in Fig. 3.1 shows how the show string and show number functions can be used to display text strings and numbers respectively. The application displays a short text message and then counts from 1 to 10. Notice how single digit numbers don't scroll while larger numbers

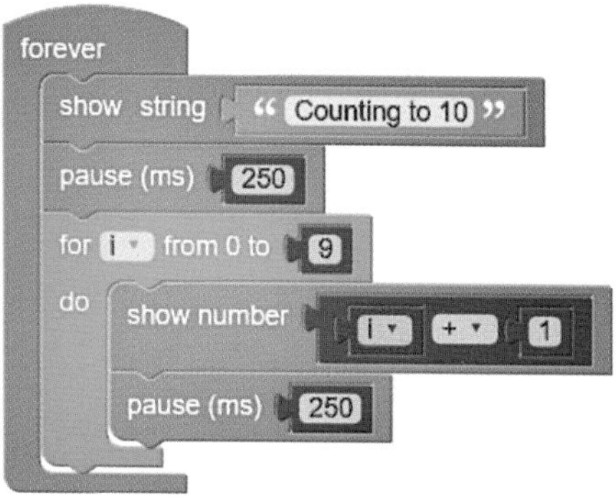

Figure 3.1 Using the show string *and* show number *functions*

(i.e. 10 or more) are scrolled from right to left across the display. The pause function introduces a short delay for comfortable viewing.

Addressing the individual LEDs

The micro:bit's display comprises 25 individual LEDs arranged in a 5×5 matrix, as shown in Fig. 3.2. The array of LEDs is organized in five columns and five rows and individual LEDs within the array can be addressed by means of their x (column) and y (row) coordinates. Thus the LED at the top left of the matrix corresponds to $x = 0$ and $y = 0$ whilst the LED at the bottom right of the display corresponds to $x = 5$, and $y = 5$. Note that the row and column numbering starts from zero (*not* 1). so the rows and columns are both numbered from 0 to 4. To turn an individual LED on or off we can use the plot and unplot code blocks.

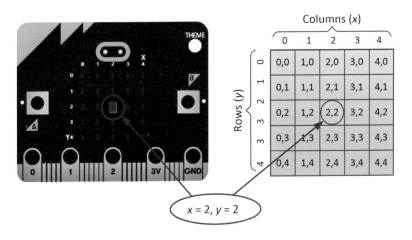

Figure 3.2 The micro:bit's LED matrix display

As an examples of using plot and unplot, the code shown in Fig. 3.3 will continuously flash the centre LED (coordinates $x = 2$, $y = 2$) whilst that shown in Fig. 3.4 continuously flashes the top left and bottom right LEDs.

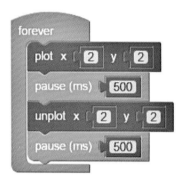

Figure 3.3 Example of using the plot *and* unplot *functions*

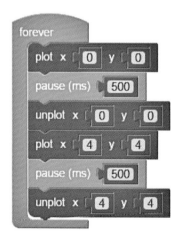

Figure 3.4 Example of using the plot *and* unplot *functions*

The micro:bit's point function will tell you whether a specified LED is currently in the on or off state. The code shown in Fig. 3.5 has exactly the same effect as that shown in Fig. 3.3.

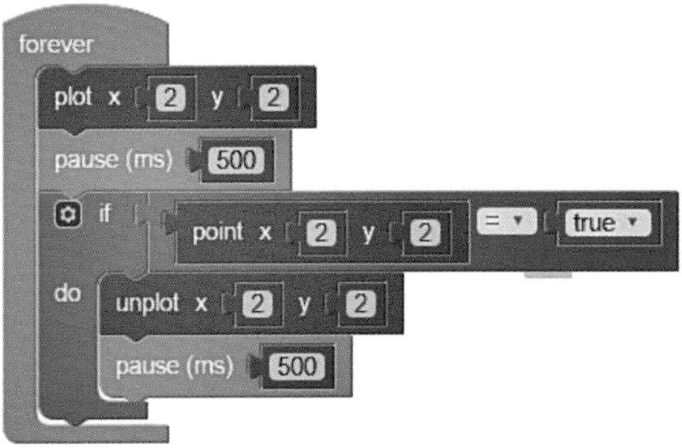

Figure 3.5 Using the point *function*

Displaying icons and images

In addition to the micro:bit's ability to address the display on an individual LED basis, Microsoft Block Editor has a neat feature that allows you to create icons and small images that can be incorporated into your applications.

The show leds function will display a pre-determined pattern on the screen for just under half a second (400ms). The pattern is created by simply placing check marks (ticks) in the required boxes within the code block. The example shown in Fig. 3.6 shows how two 45° lines can be alternately displayed. Program execution continues for as long as power is applied with the lines alternately appearing on the display.

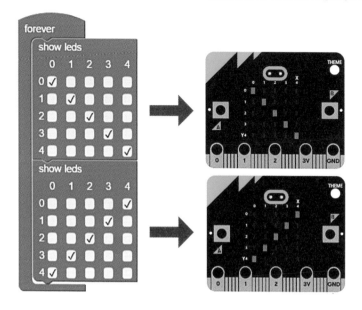

Figure 3.6 Using the show image *function*

The show image function makes it very easy to define your own icons by simply checking the required LEDs. However, you might want to have further control of your image and not just have it appear briefly. If that's the case you can make use of the show image function and use it to display an image that you've defined using the create image code block. Let's assume that you need an icon representing a power button. This can easily be created as shown in Fig. 3.7. Notice also that the position of the image (as an offset from the left of the matrix display) can be entered as a parameter (if you need to display the whole image in one go you should choose an offset of 0).

3 Using the LED display

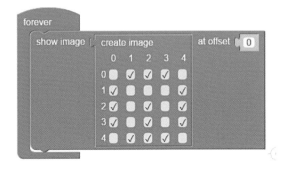

Figure 3.7 Using the show image *function*

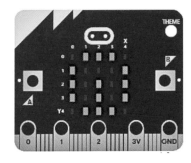

Figure 3.8 The power icon resulting from the code in Fig. 3.7

Figure 3.9 Scrolling a wavy line image across the screen

It is also possible to create a bigger image and have this scroll across the screen by at a specified rate. The example shown in Fig. 3.9 shows how a wavy line can be made to scroll continuously across the micro:bit's LED matrix display.

The micro:bit retains the state of the LED matrix display in a region of its memory known as its *display buffer*. The plot and unplot functions access this buffer directly whilst the functions that display images, text and numbers overwrite the buffer, replacing previous contents with new data.

Controlling display brightness

As its name suggests, the set brightness code block allows you to control the brightness of the LED matrix display. Brightness is determined by a parameter entered into the set brightness code block. The value entered can be anything between 0 and 255.

Fig. 3.10 shows you how this works. As the loop is executed the brightness will change in eight steps with the brightness parameter taking values ranging from 0 to 256.

Maximum brightness will result from a brightness parameter of 255, any larger value (for example, 512) will just result in maximum brightness.

Being able to control display brightness can add an extra dimension to your applications, making icons, images and messages more interesting.

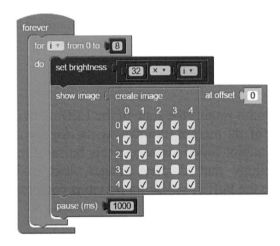

Figure 3.10 Controlling the brightness of an image

Going further—a simple micro:bit frost alarm

Our second micro:bit project is a simple device that could be extremely useful to gardeners and motorists because It provides advanced warning of frost and ice. The application makes use of the micro:bit's on-board temperature sensor.

As with our earlier dice generator project, we've used an MI:power board (see page 9) to provide power for the finished unit. However, if the alarm is to be left on for long periods it would make sense to power it from two alkaline batteries (either AAA or AA) rather than a tiny button cell.

Note how we have used an if ... do else loop in the code. We will explain how this works in Chapter 6 (see page 50).

The LED display will flash a frost warning whenever the processor's temperature falls below 2°C. Note that this will be a few degrees above the ambient temperature. Later in Chapter 9 we will show how we can sense and measure temperature with much greater accuracy using a low-cost *external* analogue temperature sensor.

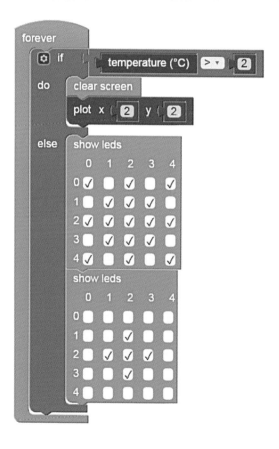

Figure 3.11 Code for the simple micro:bit frost alarm

Questions

1. How many rows and columns form the basis of the micro:bit's matrix LED display?

2. What are the *x* and *y* coordinates of the bottom left and top right LEDs of the matrix display?

3. Which micro:bit function tells you whether an LED is illuminated or not?

4. What is the purpose of the pause function when displaying a succession of images?

5. How many individual brightness levels are supported by the LED matrix display?

6. Which additional three points would need to be plotted in order to turn the icon shown in Fig. 3.12 into a closed triangle?

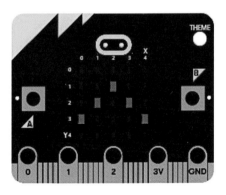

Figure 3.12 See Question 6

4

Using the buttons

What do the buttons do?

The micro:bit has two buttons that can be put to general use and a third button (at the back of the board) that's used to *reset* the processor. When the reset button is pressed, the micro:bit starts executing the code that's been downloaded to it from the beginning (the code will remain intact but any existing data will be lost). The two general purpose buttons are labelled A and B (see page 15) and these are available for you to use as you see fit.

The on button pressed function will react to the state of Button A, Button B or both A and B pressed at the same time, as illustrated in the code shown in Fig. 4.1.

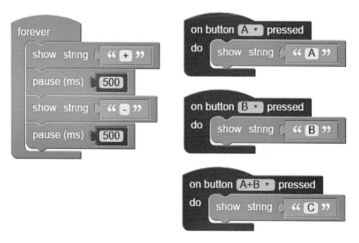

Figure 4.1 Using the micro:bit's button inputs

4 Using the buttons

When a button is pressed, the action (or actions) to be performed are inserted in the slot marked do. Just click and drag the required block into position.

In Fig. 4.1 we simply wanted to indicate which of the buttons has been pressed. A will appear when Button A has been pressed, B will appear when Button B has been pressed and C will appear when both buttons (A and B) have been pressed at the same time (on the virtual micro:bit a separate A+B button has been provided (see Fig. 2.10) so that you can simulate this). You thus have three possibilities for button inputs.

The code shown in Fig. 4.2 provides you with an example of doing something a little more useful with button inputs. Button A will set the display to full brightness (the default state) while Button B will dim the display. Note that the display will remain in whatever state has been selected until one of the buttons is pressed again.

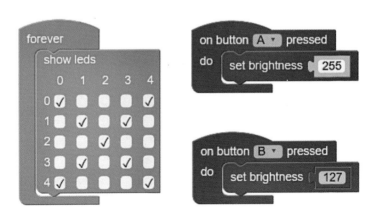

Figure 4.2 Using buttons to set the display brightness

Counting with micro:bit

Earlier on page 17 we showed how the micro:bit could be used to count a number of button presses. Now let's look at a more complex example of a counting application in which all three buttons are used. The code shown in Fig. 4.3 counts up when Button A is pressed and counts down when Button B is pressed. When both buttons are pressed the count is reset to zero. Counting up is achieved by adding 1 to the value of count whilst counting down is achieved by subtracting 1 from the value of count.

Notice how, within the forever loop we first initialise the value of count (by setting it to zero). This is good practice but not essential. Notice also how, because the test condition has been set to true, the while ... do loop continues forever. We will return to this important point in a later chapter.

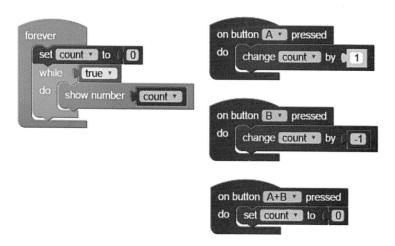

Figure 4.3 The improved counting application

Waiting to start and waiting to stop

A particularly useful application for a button is that of starting or stopping the execution of a block of code. For example, waiting for a user to press a button before something happens or waiting for a user to release a button before moving on to some other action.

The code shown in Fig. 4.4 will continuously display a '?' character but, if Button A is pressed *and kept held down* the LED will display a '*' symbol. When Button A is released the display will revert to a '?' character. If you need to use something like this in your own code just replace the code block in the do notch.

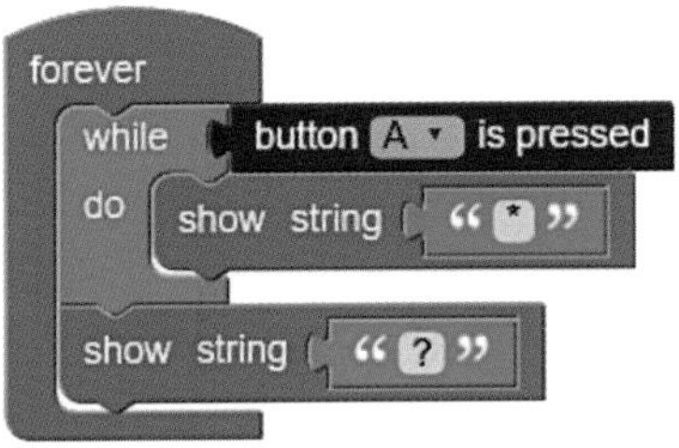

Figure 4.4 Code that waits for a button to be pressed

Going further—a reaction timer

Our third micro:bit project is a fun gadget that takes the form of a personal reaction timer. The program starts by displaying a single dot in the centre of the LED matrix. It then waits until the user operates Button A (notice the test condition, not button A is pressed. As long as Button A is *not* pressed the micro:bit executes an empty loop.

When, eventually Button A is pressed execution then continues with the code that immediately follows the while … loop. The screen is cleared and the program executes a random delay of between 0 and 4.5s (9 × 500 = 4,500ms). Thereafter, a random dot appears on the display and the time is noted. This is the prompt for the user to press Button B. After a few 100ms delay (caused by the user's reactions not being immediate) the user presses Button B and the delay, user time, is then calculated and displayed, scrolling the value (in milliseconds) across the display. The process then repeats indefinitely.

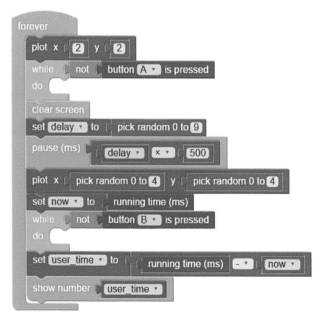

Figure 4.5 Reaction timer code

Questions

1. What is the purpose of the micro:bit's reset button and where is it located?

2. Is it possible to detect both buttons being simultaneously pressed and how is this achieved with the virtual micro:bit?

3. How is it possible to use a button to control the micro:bit's display brightness?

4. How can the change ... by code block be used as the basis of (a) an up-counter and (b) a down-counter?

5. In the block of code shown in Fig. 4.6, what will appear on the LED matrix display when (a) Button A is held down and (b) when Button A is released?

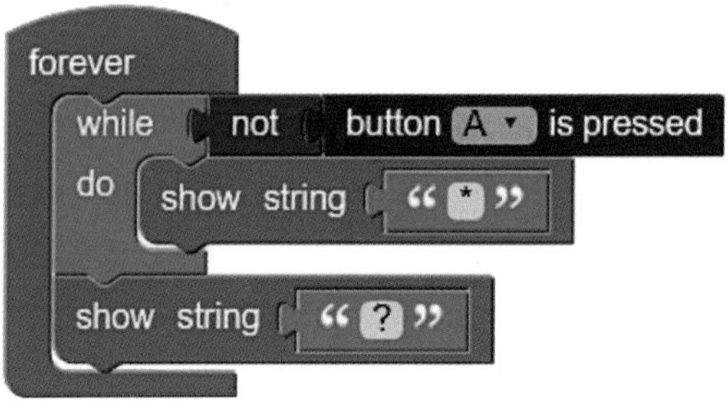

Figure 4.6 See Question 5

5

Loops

What does a loop do?

A loop is simply a repeated section of code. Because the execution of a loop depends on the outcome of a particular condition, a loop may execute once, several times, indefinitely or not at all! There a several different types of loop so let's take another look at those that you've already met before we introduce some new ones.

The forever *loop*

Everything placed inside a forever loop executes indefinitely (or at least until the micro:bit's power is switched off). Since we often need our code to run continuously (i.e. not just once or a limited number of times) we usually place our code inside an outer forever loop. Fig. 5.1 shows a program that uses a forever loop to continuously display the program's running time in seconds.

The while … do *loop*

The while … do loop will continuously execute the commands contained in it as long as the specified *test condition* remains *true*. If the test condition evaluates to *false* the loop is exited and program execution continues with the statement that immediately follows the while … do block. Fig. 5.2 shows an example in the form of a simple egg timer.

5 Loops

Figure 5.1 Code that display the time for which a program is running

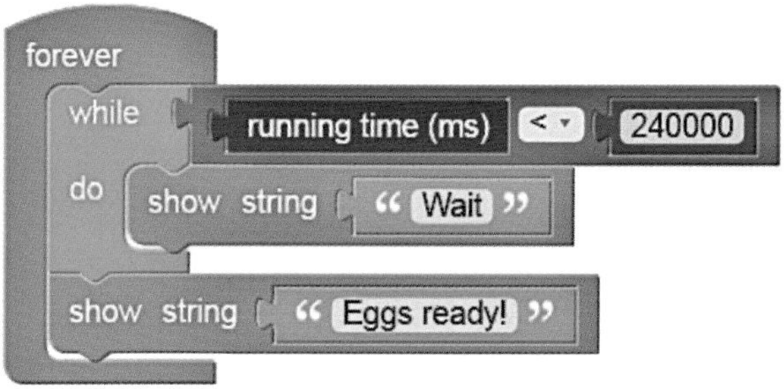

Figure 5.2 A simple egg timer using a while … do *loop*

In the code shown in Fig. 5.2, the first while … do loop tests the current value of running time. If this is less than 240000 (corresponding to an elapsed time of four minutes) the expression evaluates to true. In that case, a 'Wait' message is continuously scrolled across the matrix display.

If the elapsed time exceeds 240000 the expression evaluates to false and execution continues with the next command which displays the 'Eggs ready!' message. Note that the expression used in each of the test conditions must be taken from the Logic code block library and not from the Maths code block library. The reason for this is that the test condition must evaluate to a Boolean logical expression (i.e. either true or false) , not a numerical value.

The for ... do *block*

The for ... do block allows you to repeat a block of code a predetermined number of times. The loop *index* is a *variable* that keeps track of the number of times that the loop has been executed. By default, the i is used for this variable but you can change this to a variable of your choice. You can set the number of times that the loop executes by changing the value given (currently this defaults to 4). Here's an example that moves a point across the matrix display, starting in the top-left and ending in the bottom-right. Notice how one for ... do loop is nested inside another. Each time the outer loop is executed the inner loop is executed five times. The column number is used as the index for the inner loop. Because it will help you understand how loop nesting works it is well worth testing this example for yourself.

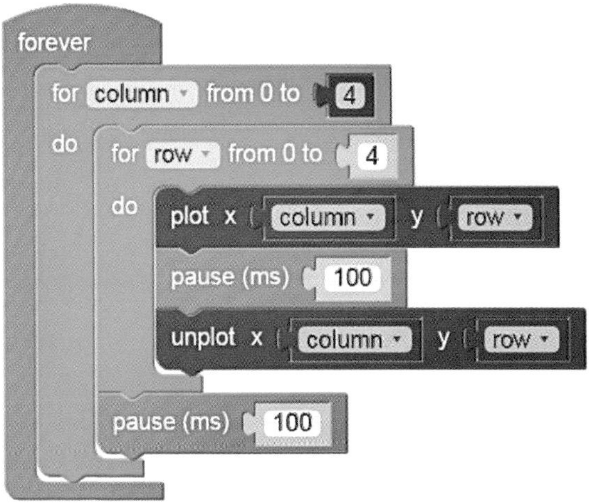

Figure 5.3 Example of nested for ... do *loops*

The repeat ... do *block*

The repeat ... do block provides you with a very easy way of repeating one or more code block commands. It simply executes the snapped code the number of times specified. The default number of times is currently four but you can change this to any number that you require. The example shown in Fig. 5.4 flashes two characters on the LED matrix display before scrolling a 'Ready!' message.

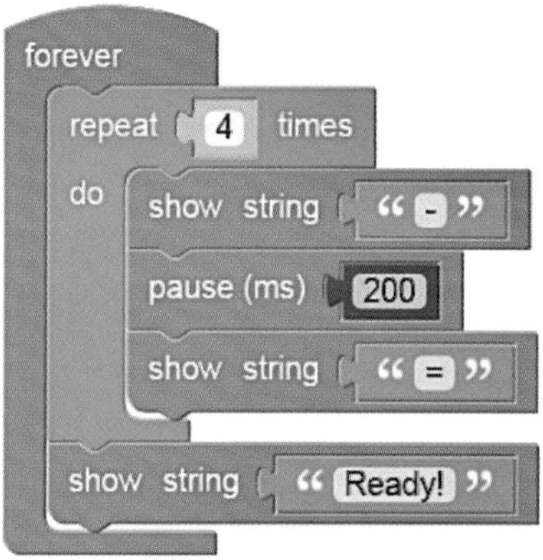

Figure 5.4 Using the repeat ... do *block*

Going further—a simple theft alarm

Our fourth micro:bit project provides you with a simple method of protecting your property by generating an alarm signal whenever it is moved. You could place this gadget in a bag or suitcase or attach it to something more valuable such as a computer or jewellery box. When the protected device is moved the alarm will sound. The application makes use of the micro:bit's built-in accelerometer which is able to detect motion in all three axes; *x, y* and *z*. In this case we are just going to use the *y-*axis but since the movement can be positive or negative with respect to the reference plane we must base our test condition on the absolute value of acceleration rather than its actual numerical value (which can be either positive or negative). When acceleration exceeds the set

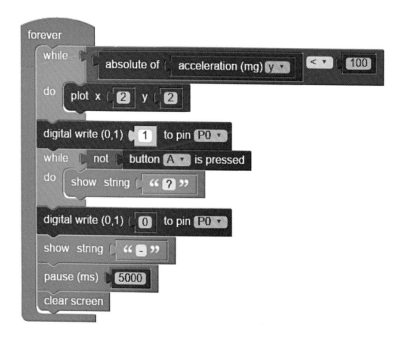

Figure 5.5 Code for the simple theft alarm

value (we chose 100 so as to make the device reasonably sensitive) execution passes from the first while ... do loop and a logic 1 (high) will be sent to a piezoelectric sounder using the digital write code block. The code then waits in the second while ... do loop until the user presses Button A. When this happens the second loop exits and a logic 0 (low) is sent to the piezoelectric sounder. There is then a short five second delay which allows the gadget to be repositioned before execution resumes with the first while ... do loop and thus re-arming the alarm.

The piezoelectric sounder is available from a number of suppliers but must be a low-current type that emits continuous sound and should be rated for operation from a 3V input at a current of less than 5 mA. The sounder is connected to the micro:bit with the positive lead taken to Pin-0 and the negative connection taken to GND (see page 47).

For test purposes, connection can be made using crocodile clips (as shown in Fig. 5.6) or by means of an edge connector (as shown in Fig. 5.7). Edge connectors are available from various sources (the one shown in Fig. 5.7 is from Kitronik). Note that the piezo sounder is polarised and must be connected with the correct polarity. Take care not to short circuit Pin-0 to GND or to any of the micro:bit's other pins.

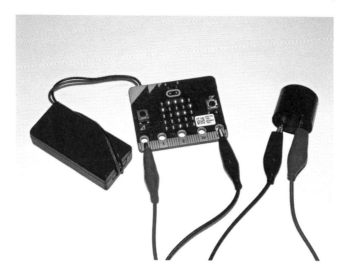

Figure 5.6 Testing the micro:bit theft alarm

Figure 5.7 Using an edge connector with the micro:bit

Questions

1. What are the two states that a Boolean expression can evaluate to?

2. In what units is micro:bit running time expressed?

3. Is it possible to nest one loop within the body of another? Explain your answer.

4. In Fig. 5.8 what is the name of the variable used for the loop index?

5. What does the code shown in Fig. 5.8 do and what is the purpose of the empty while ... do block?

6. In Fig. 5.8 what are the first and last numerical values displayed on the LED matrix?

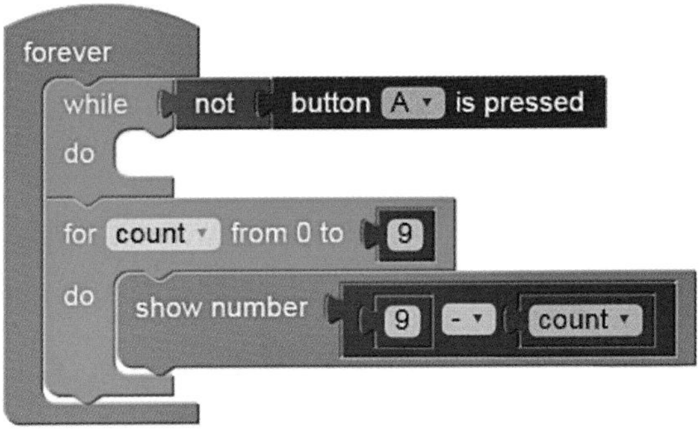

Figure 5.8 See Questions 4, 5 and 6

Decisions

Why do we need to make decisions?

Humans make decisions every day. If the sun is shining we might take a walk. If it looks like it might rain we might pick up an umbrella. We mentally process many thousands of such questions every day without even realising it.

Sometimes its easy to make a choice. Sometimes it can be more difficult. For example, if we finish work early, and if we have some spare cash, and if the pub's open, and if it's not raining, we might decide to out for a drink. The eventual outcome, whether to go out for a drink, depends on a number of criteria being met. If any of them isn't met we just stay home and put our feet up!

Our micro:bit applications also need to make decisions based on what's going on at the time. We've already shown how while ... do can execute code when a condition is met (i.e. when a logical expression evaluates to true or false, as required), now it's time to look at a more complex construct that will provide you with means of executing a number of possible outcomes contained within a single block.

The if ... do *logic block*

The if ... do logic block exists in a number of different variants so we will start with the most simple of them in which a condition is tested and, if it is found to be true, the enclosed code block (or blocks) will be executed. However, if the condition evaluates to false none of the blocks will be executed and execution simply moves on to the block of code that follows the if ... do block.

A simple example of if ... do logic is shown in Fig. 6.1. The code fragment tests the state of the Boolean value triggered, and if this evaluates to true an appropriate message is scrolled on the LED matrix display.

Configuring the if ... do *logic block*

To configure the if ... do logic block so that it can perform more complex decisions you can click on the cog-shaped icon shown at the top left of the code block. This will provide you with two further options in the form of else if and else that can be dragged and slotted into the if ... do block, as shown in Fig. 6.2. When this is done the code shown in the main editor window will be updated in order to reflect and changes that you've made.

You now have some several new if ... do constructs to play with, such as if ... do ... else and if ... do else if. The examples that follow should help if this is sounding a little complex.

The if ... do else *logic block*

The if ... do else loop will test a condition and, if it found to be true, the enclosed statement (or statements) will be executed (as before). However, if the condition is found to be false the code positioned against else will be executed. This will allow you test a condition and then execute one section of code or another depending on the outcome.

Figure 6.1 Simple example of if ... do *logic*

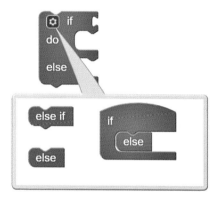

Figure 6.2 Configuring the if ... do *logic block*

Earlier in Chapter 3 we used an if ... do else code block in a simple frost alarm that displays a flashing warning on the matrix LED display whenever the micro:bit's temperature falls below 2°C.

It is important to be aware that you can edit an if ... do else block, adding any further conditions that you need to test for or removing any conditions if you don't need them. Fig. 6.3 shows how multiple else if blocks can be added before reaching the block's final else statement. In practice you can add as many else if blocks as you need.

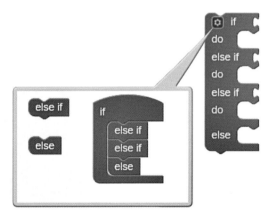

Figure 6.3 Building a more complex if ... do *logic block*

The if ... do else if else *logic block*

The final variant of the if ... do logic might sound something of a mouthful but it allows you to test for multiple conditions and execute different sections of code according to the outcomes. The code shown in Fig. 6.4 is a simple fridge alarm application that can be used to check the temperature inside a fridge, displaying messages to warn the owner if there's a problem.

Testing Boolean conditions

You might have noticed that we've used the < (less than) comparison in the code shown in Fig. 6.4. Usefully, the Microsoft Block Editor provides you with several other comparisons that can be selected from a drop-down list that appears when you click on the small down arrow inside the comparison operator box.

The result of the Boolean comparison operation will be either true or false and this, in turn, will determine the action of the if ... do logic block (i.e. whether the do code will be executed, or not). Table 6.1 summarises the six available comparison operations.

Finally, the code in Fig. 6.5 provides you with an example of using Boolean comparisons of two randomly generated numbers, a and b. The program runs continuously with a pause after each result is checked. The outcome of the comparison appears as a text message that scrolls across the LED matrix display. This message indicates whether the first randomly generated number is greater than, less than, or equal to the second randomly generated number.

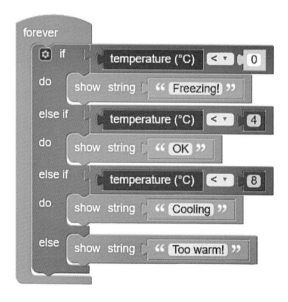

Figure 6.4 The micro:bit fridge alarm

Symbol	Meaning
=	Is equal to
!=	Is not equal to
<	Is less than
>	Is greater than
<=	Is less than or equal to
>=	Is greater than or equal to

Table 6.1 Boolean comparison operators

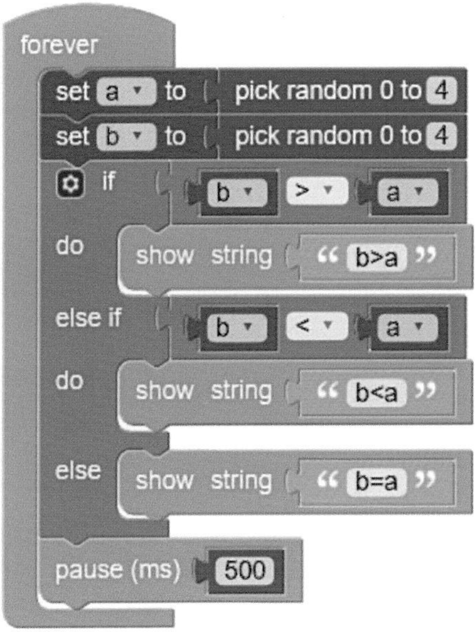

Figure 6.5 Example of making Boolean comparison operations

Going further—a micro:bit direction finder

Our fifth micro:bit project is a simple direction finder that will indicate the micro:bit's orientation using the cardinal points of the compass; north (N), east (E), south (S) and west (W). The project makes use of the micro:bit's built in magnetometer and its LED matrix display.

The code for the micro:bit direction finder is shown in Fig. 6.6. The first logic block sets a variable, direction, to the micro:bit's current compass heading. This will be a value in the range 0 to 359°. The value obtained is then used in the test conditions contained in a compound if … do else if else logic block.

The first Boolean comparison tests whether the value of direction is either greater than or equal to 315° or less

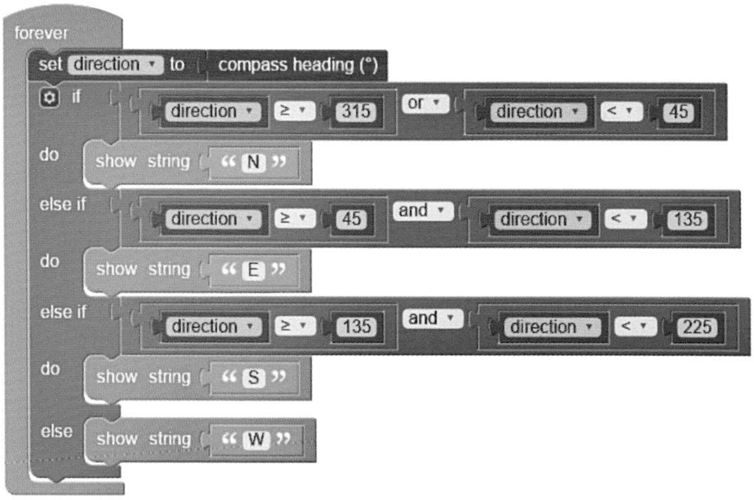

Figure 6.6 The micro:bit direction finder

than 45°. If the condition is found to be true the micro:bit will display 'N' and then exit the logic block. The second Boolean comparison tests whether the value of direction is greater than or equal to 45° and less than 135°. If the condition is found to be true the micro:bit will display 'E' and then exit the logic block. The third Boolean comparison tests whether the value of direction is greater than or equal to 135° and less than 225°. If the condition is found to be true the micro:bit will display 'S' and then exit the logic block. There is no need for a fourth comparison test because if the first three tests fail the only remaining possibility is that direction has a value between 225° and 315° in which case the display will show 'W' and exit the logic block.

When first run, the magnetometer needs to be calibrated and you will be prompted to calibrate the sensor by moving the board around in a circle in order to illuminate all of the LEDs around the periphery of the display, draw a complete circle (see Fig. 6.7). When this process has been completed the sensor will be ready for use. Note that to obtain an accurate bearing you will need to hold the board horizontally and keep it still for a few seconds. Indications may be inaccurate when used in proximity to magnets and ferromagnetic materials generally. Finally, it is important to perform the initial calibration with the intended power source connected (particularly if the power source is the MI:power board). This board is in very close proximity to the sensor and can result in a constant error if calibration is performed before the power board is attached to the micro:bit.

Figure 6.7 Calibrating the micro:bit direction finder

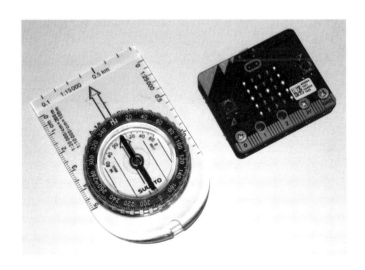

Figure 6.8 Checking the direction finder against a compass

Questions

1. What is the result of each of the following Boolean comparisons when the values of variable a and b are respectively 3 and 5?
   (a) a = b   (b) a > b   (c) a < b   (d) b > a
   (e) b < a   (f) a != b   (g) b ≥ a   (h) a = a

2. What is the purpose of else within an if ... do else logical block?

3. Is it possible to have more than one else if statement within an if ... do else if logical block?

4. What is wrong with the code shown in Fig. 6.9 and why does this code not execute correctly? Explain your answer.

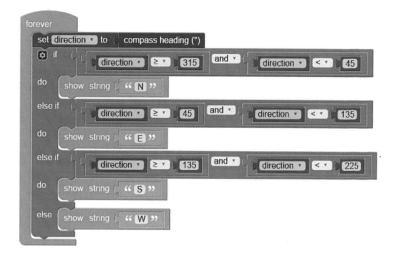

Figure 6.9 See Question 4

Digital I/O

Which pins to use?

Digital I/O is extremely straightforward on the micro:bit but the question of which of the digital I/O pins to use is a tricky one. It might at first appear that there's plenty of pins to choose from but it's important to remember that many (indeed, most) of these are taken up with existing functions, such as the LED matrix display or accelerometer chips. In fact, there are only five inputs that can be used for digital I/O without having to worry about the impact on other micro:bit functions!

If you are prepared to sacrifice the LED display then you have six more possibilities; pins 3, 4, 6, 7, 9, and 10. In addition, if you don't need to make use of the two buttons (Button A and Button B) two more pins become available, pins 5 and 11.

Since the SPI bus uses pins 13, 14, and 15 whilst I^2C makes use of pins 19 and 20. It is unwise to use any of these pins if you plan to make use of these two bus standards. As a result, the preferred digital I/O pins are pins 8 and 16 closely followed by pins 0, 1 and 2.

The first three of these are brought out to large pads whilst the remaining pair are available on the smaller pins and must be accessed by means of a ready-made edge connector such as those supplied by Kitronik and Utronix (see Figs. 7.1 and 7.2).

Figure 7.1 The Kitronik micro:bit edge connector

Figure 7.2 The Utronix micro:bit edge connector

Connecting buttons and switches

It's easy to connect an external button or a switch to the micro:bit but it's important to remember that, when the switch is operated, the voltage change must be sufficient for it to cause a change in logic level, from a 0 (low) to a 1 (high) and vice versa. A high state is normally taken to be equivalent to a voltage of +3V (or near) whilst a low state is a voltage of 0V (or near).

In order to ensure that sufficient change takes place we use pull-up or pull-down resistors, like those shown in Fig. 7.3. Note that the micro:bit has internal *pull-up* and *pull-down* resistors but, because we don't want to forget that they are there, we will duplicate them externally. Thus, in the active-low input arrangement shown in (a), when the normally open contacts of S1 are closed the input state will change from a logical 1 to logical 0. Conversely, in the

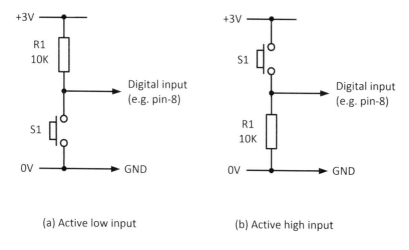

(a) Active low input   (b) Active high input

Figure 7.3 Connecting switches to the micro:bit's digital inputs

active-high input arrangement shown in (b), when the normally open contacts of S1 are closed the input state will change from a logical 0 to logical 1. Finally, it is important to note that you should never exceed the nominal 3V supply to these two circuits. Anything much more than 3V will damage the micro:bit!

Connecting output devices

Output devices consist of LEDs, relays, motors, sounders, etc. Unfortunately most of these require voltages and currents that are well beyond the capability of the micro:bit. Because of this some form of interface will be required along with a power source that's capable of delivering the voltage and current required.

Output driver circuits

A typical LED driver circuit is shown in Fig. 7.4. This circuit uses a MOSFET transistor operating as a switch, conducting heavily when the gate voltage goes high. The value of R2 sets the current flowing through the LED (approximately 10mA with the value shown when operating from 5V). Fig. 7.5 shows a typical relay driver. The relay can be any miniature type suitable for operation from a voltage of between 5V and 12V. A typical 5V relay has a coil resistance of around 70Ω and operates with a current of about 70mA (well in excess of the micro:bit's capabilities!).

Note that, since both of these driver circuits require active high inputs for the transistors to conduct (i.e. to switch 'on'), a logic 1 (high) from the micro:bit is required to turn the LED on or operate the relay.

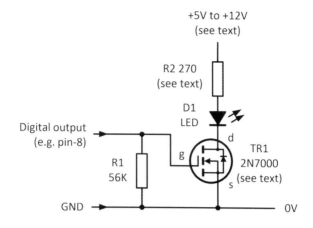

Figure 7.4 A typical MOSFET LED driver

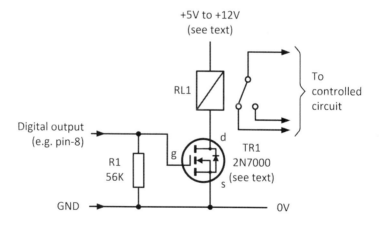

Figure 7.5 A typical MOSFET relay driver

An alternative to constructing your own relay interface is that of using a ready-made relay module. These are widely available at low cost and are often designed for use with Arduino or Raspberry Pi boards but can be used with the micro:bit. Such boards are often compatible with both 3V and 5V logic systems. Fig. 7.6 shows a two-channel relay module that uses miniature changeover relays whilst Fig. 7.7 shows a two-channel solid-state relay module capable of handling mains voltage loads of up to 500W.

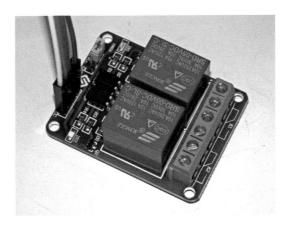

Figure 7.6 A two-channel relay module

Figure 7.7 A two-channel solid-state relay module

Supplying power to interface circuits

One problematic feature of the micro:bit (at least as far as the electronic enthusiast is concerned) is the absence of a +5V pin on the board's edge connector. This is a particular concern when an interface circuit requires a 5V supply. There are, however, a number of ways of overcoming this problem, as shown in Fig. 7.8.

The arrangement shown in Fig. 7.8(d) derives its power from a small low-cost USB battery and it is ideal for projects that need additional interface circuitry. The 5V output is invariably protected and regulated and the capacity of the battery (typically 4500 mA/h, or more) is sufficient to provide power for many hours of continuous operation.

The dual outputs available from the USB battery make it possible to deliver 5V to the micro:bit as well as a separate 5V supply to the interface. When using this arrangement it is important to ensure that the edge connector GPIO signals remain at 3V logic levels. Note also that some 'automatic' chargers will turn off when the current demand placed on them is small. If that's the case, it might be necessary to place an additional resistive load across the output. A 0.5W resistor of 68Ω to 100Ω will usually be adequate for this purpose.

Extra pins can easily be added to the Kitronik micro:bit edge connector in order to provide 5V and GND for an interface module, as shown in Fig. 7.12 on page 69. These pins can provide power for relay modules and other boards that use 5V logic or need 5V to operate relays and other devices. The example on page 69 shows how this is done.

7 Digital I/O

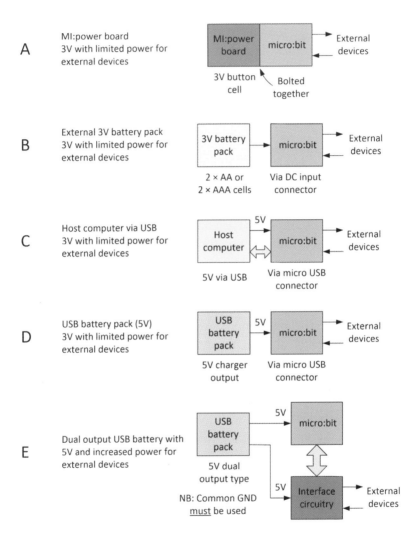

A MI:power board
   3V with limited power for
   external devices

B External 3V battery pack
   3V with limited power for
   external devices

C Host computer via USB
   3V with limited power for
   external devices

D USB battery pack (5V)
   3V with limited power for
   external devices

E Dual output USB battery with
   5V and increased power for
   external devices

Figure 7.8 Power options for external devices

Reading from and writing to digital I/O

Reading from a digital input is achieved using the digital read pin logic block. The pin to be read is selected from the drop-down list which provides you with the choice of available uncommitted digital I/O pins.

Writing to a digital output is just as simple. The digital write logic block allows you to output a logic 0 (low) or logic 1 (high) to the pin of your choice. A simple example of reading the state of an external button and writing to an external LED is shown in Fig. 7.9. The corresponding interface circuit is shown in Fig. 7.10 together with the prototype breadboard layout in Fig. 7.11. The 5V supply is derived from additional pins fitted to the Kitronik edge connector board (see page 69).

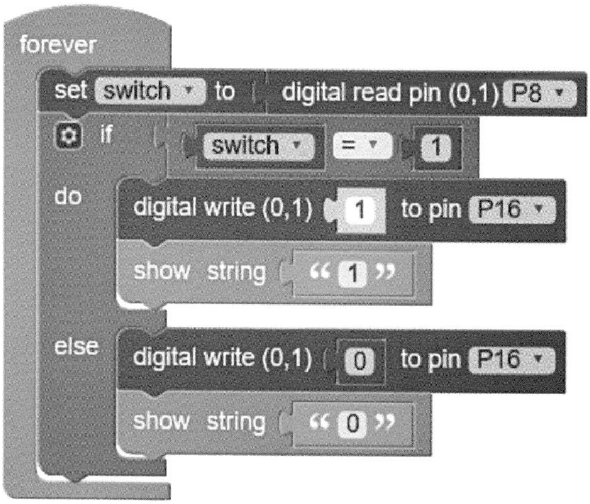

Figure 7.9 Example of nested digital read and digital write logic

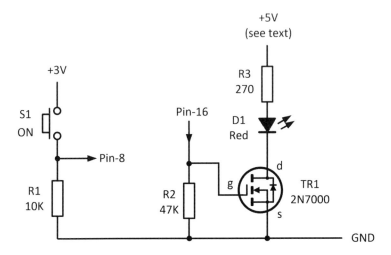

Figure 7.10 The button and LED interface circuit

Figure 7.11 The prototype board layout for the circuit in Fig. 7.10

Figure 7.12 Connections to the Kitronik edge connector (see page 60)

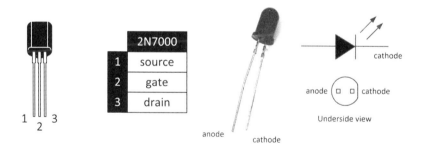

Figure 7.13 Pin connections for TR1 and D1

The pin connections for TR1 and D1 are shown in Fig. 7.13. If you build and test this simple interface you will find that D1 will become illuminated whenever S1 pressed.

Going further—a micro:bit intruder alarm

Our sixth micro:bit project takes the form of an intruder alarm based on a closed loop which will normally comprise a number of magnetic switches secured to doors and windows. Once set, if the loop is broken, or if the wiring is cut, the alarm will be triggered.

The circuit of the intruder alarm is shown in Fig. 7.14. The inputs to the micro:bit are:

- pin-2 (a high state to *set* the alarm)

- pin-12 (a low state to indicate that the loop has been cut or that the contacts have opened on one of the magnetic switches).

Both of these inputs are at 3V logic levels.

The outputs from the micro:bit are:

- pin-16 (a high to show that the alarm has been set)

- pin-8 (a high to sound the alarm).

The *set* state is indicated using a green LED while the *triggered* state is indicated using a red LED.

Current for the LEDs and the alarm sounder is derived from a 5V supply using an arrangement similar to that used in the previous example. If further outputs are required in addition to the sounder a relay module (see Fig. 7.7) can be incorporated into the alarm and its input taken from the drain of TR2. This will permit a mains load, such as security lighting or a siren, to be used.

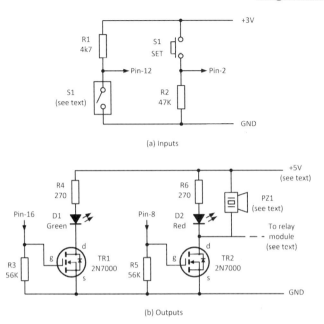

Figure 7.14 The intruder alarm circuit

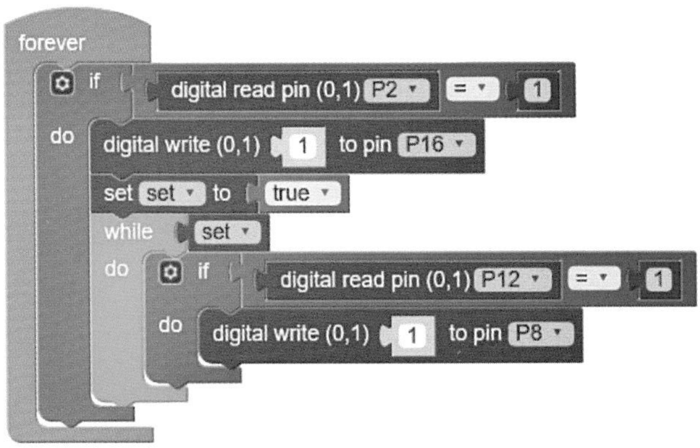

Figure 7.15 The intruder alarm code

Questions

1. What voltage levels are used to represent the micro:bit's logical states 0 and 1, respectively?

2. What voltage level is often used by many relay and other small modules designed for use with microcontrollers?

3. In Fig. 7.16, what logic state needs to be present at pin-16 in order to operate the motor, M1?

4. In Fig. 7.16, what logic state appears at pin-0 when S1 is pressed?

5. In Fig. 7.16, what is the purpose of:
(a) R1 and (b) R2?

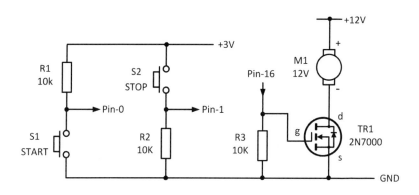

Figure 7.16 See questions 3, 4 and 5

8

Analogue I/O

What are analogue signals?

As you saw in the previous chapter, digital signals can only exist in one of two discrete states (i.e. high and low or on and off). Analogue signals, on the other hand, are continuously variable. In order to work with analogue signals the micro:bit has a built-in analogue to digital converter (ADC).

The micro:bit's ADC accepts analogue inputs over the range 0 to +3.3V and converts them to corresponding 10-bit digital codes. This means that an analogue input of 0V will be represented by a binary value of 0000000000 while a value of approximately 3.3V will be represented by a binary value of 1111111111 (corresponding to a range from 0 to 1023 when expressed in decimal). Each increment in output from the ADC corresponds to a change of (3.3/1024) or approximately 32mV. This is the smallest change in level that the micro:bit can recognise.

Using analog read

In order to read the analogue voltage present at one of the micro:bit's available analogue I/O pins (pin-0, pin-1 and pin-2) Microsoft Block Editor provides you with the analog read function. The value returned from the function can be assigned to a variable of our choice. For example, input, as shown in Fig. 8.1. Note that we also need to specify the analogue pin that we are reading.

8 Analogue I/O

In order to test the code shown in Fig. 8.1 you can connect a variable potentiometer (of 10kΩ, or more) as shown in Fig. 8.2(a) and Fig. 8.3. You will find that the micro:bit will display a reading close to zero (it might actually read 1 or 2) at one extreme setting of the control and 1023 at the other.

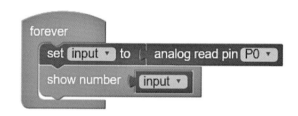

Figure 8.1 Using the analog read pin *code block*

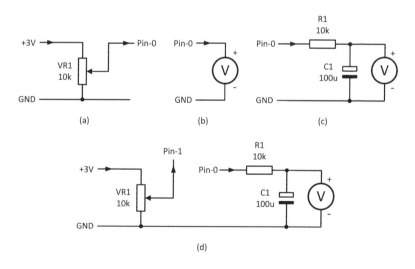

Figure 8.2 Testing the micro:bit's analogue I/O

Figure 8.3 Connecting the potentiometer the micro:bit'.
The slider (yellow wire) is taken to the analogue input pin

Using analog write

In order to output an analogue voltage from one of the micro:bit's available I/O pins (pin-0, pin-1 and pin-2) Microsoft Code Blocks provides you with the analog write function. The code shown in Fig.8.4 can be used together with the circuit shown in Fig.8.2(b) in order to output an analogue voltage in the range 0V to +3.3V. The *mean* voltage at the output is determined by the value written to the pin (511 in this case).

Notice that we just used the phrase 'mean voltage'. This is rather important because the micro:bit is not actually capable to producing a true analogue output. Instead it

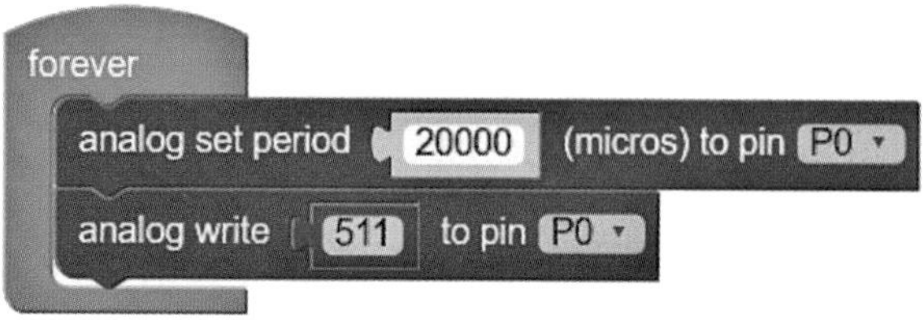

Figure 8.4 Using analog write *to output an analogue voltage*

produces a digital waveform that is pulse width modulated (PWM). The waveform has a constant amplitude (approximately 3.3V) and a duty cycle that depends on the data value that's being written to the pin. A duty cycle of 100% (i.e. a continuous high state output) will result from a data value of 1023 whilst a duty cycle of 0% (a continuous low output) will result from a data value of 0. A 50% duty cycle (where the high and low times are identical) will correspond to a data value of 512.

Fig. 8.5 shows the output waveform at pin-0 for a 30% duty cycle (corresponding to a mean output of just over 1V) while the Fig. 8.6 shows the output waveform at pin-0 with a 70% duty cycle (corresponding to an output of approximately 2.2V). In order to produce a more constant voltage level (rather than a series of pulses) we can smooth the output using a simple C-R low-pass filter, like that shown in Fig. 8.2(c). Fig, 8.7 shows how this affects the output waveform. Note that, in all cases, the output is at a high-impedance level and, although the voltage will appear reasonably accurate when measured using a digital voltmeter or an oscilloscope, it will *not* be correct when a low resistance load is present at the output.

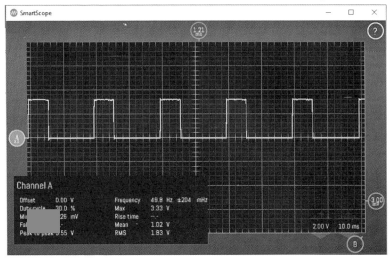

Figure 8.5 Analogue output with 30% duty cycle

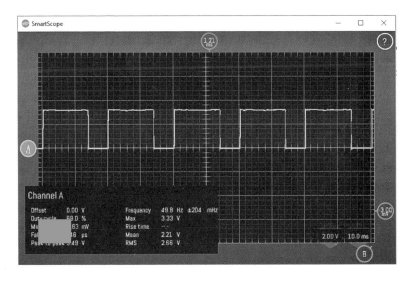

Figure 8.6 Analogue output with 70% duty cycle

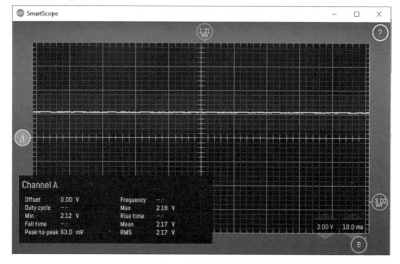

Figure 8.7 Effect of the C-R low-pass filter in Fig. 8.2(c)

Reading and writing analogue data

You may sometimes find that you need to read and write analogue data in the *same* application. For example, when using a variable potentiometer to control the speed of a small d.c. motor.

This can be easily done using code based on the example shown in the Fig. 8.8. In this case we are using pin-0 for analogue (PWM) output and pin-1 for analogue input.

The code example shown in Fig. 8.8 can be quite instructive. Using the arrangement shown in Fig. 8.2(d) (and with a voltmeter connected to the output) you will find that the output voltage level can be easily adjusted to any desired voltage in the range 0V to +3.3V.

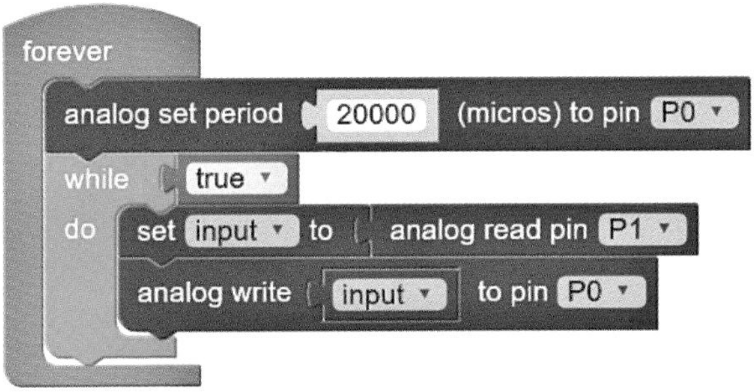

Figure 8.8 Reading and writing analogue data

The analog set period block is used to configure the period of the Pulse Width Modulation (PWM) on the specified analogue pin (e.g. pin-0, pin-1 or pin-2).

Determining the input and output voltage

The micro:bit ADC input voltage can be calculated from:

$$V_{in} = input \times \frac{3.3}{1023}$$

Example

If a value of 795 is returned by the analog read pin function, the corresponding voltage will be given by:

$$V_{in} = 795 \times \frac{3.3}{1023} = 2.56V$$

Where input is the variable returned from the analog read pin code block. Note that input can take a value between 0 and 1023. In the analog write pin code block the data value, output, to write to the ADC is given by:

$$output = V_{out} \times \frac{1023}{3.3}$$

Where V_{out} is the required mean output voltage. Note that V_{out} can take a value between 0V and +3.3V.

Example

If an output of 0.5V is required, the data value to use will be given by:

$$output = 0.5 \times \frac{1023}{3.3} = 155$$

Going further—a micro:bit battery checker

Our seventh micro:bit project involves the construction of a micro:bit battery checker. This handy gadget is designed to test conventional 1.5V alkaline cells. In order to provide you with a meaningful indication of the state of a cell it is placed 'on-load'. In this condition, the measured voltage will be in excess of 1.5V for a new battery falling to less than 1.2V for a battery that is in imminent need of replacement.

The circuit of the micro:bit battery checker is shown in Fig. 8.9. A 1N4148 diode, D1, is used to protect the micro:bit against inadvertent reverse polarity while the resistor, R1, provides the test load.

The value of R1 (15Ω, 0.5W) is chosen so as to demand a current of typically between 30mA and 50mA from the cell on test. After inserting the battery an appropriate text message will be scrolled against the micro:bit's LED matrix display.

The threshold ranges used in the if ... do ... else logic block (see Fig. 8.10) were chosen so that they provide four ranges of voltage:

- Greater than 1.5V: 'Good'
- Between 1.35V and 1.5V: 'Fair'
- Between 1.2V and 1.35V: 'Poor'
- Less than 1.2V: 'Bad'.

If you need to test other types of cell, for example NiCd or NiMh batteries, the threshold values can be easily changed.

The micro:bit battery checker interface can be a assembled on a small piece of strip board, as shown in Fig. 8.11. The complete prototype on test is shown in Fig. 8.12. An AA cell-holder (which will accommodate both AA and AAA batteries) can be connected to the strip board using a small terminal block. In order to make cell insertion and removal easier, the cell holder can be easily modified by cutting away some of the plastic moulding.

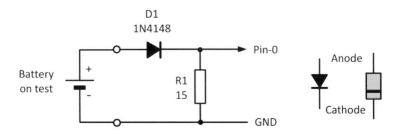

Figure 8.9 Circuit for the micro:bit battery checker interface

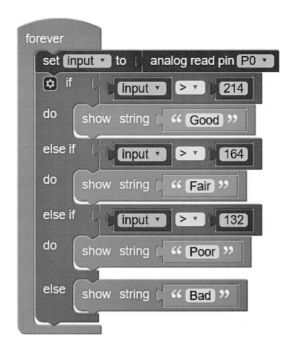

Figure 8.10 Code for the micro:bit battery checker

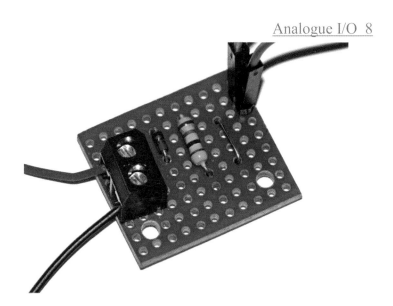

Figure 8.11 The strip board layout for the battery checker interface

Figure 8.12 The completed prototype micro:bit battery checker

Questions

1. Which three micro:bit I/O pins can be used for analogue input and output?

2. Expressed in bits, what is the resolution of the micro:bit's ADC?

3. How many different analogue voltage levels can be recognised by the micro:bit?

4. What is the smallest change in analogue voltage that the micro:bit can detect?

5. Which code block allows you to read an analogue voltage present at pin-1?

6. Can the micro:bit produce a true analogue output? Explain your answer.

7. If a mean output voltage of 2.2V is required what value needs to be written to one of the micro:bit's analogue output pins?

Sensing temperature

Temperature sensors

Being able to sense and respond to changes in temperature is an important requirement in many microcontroller applications. Fortunately, temperature sensing is easy with a range of popular low-cost three-pin TO92 packaged temperature sensors like the TMP36 and LM35. These devices are very easily interfaced to the micro:bit's analogue inputs, as we will see later.

Both devices provide an analogue output that varies on a linear basis at 10mV per degree Centigrade. However, there's a notable difference in the temperature range covered and the scaling that needs to be applied when converting raw data from these two sensors to temperature output that can be displayed in °C on the micro:bit.

Using the TMP34, 35 and 36 sensors

The TMP34, 35 and 36 sensors are members of a family of devices that together are capable of operating over a temperature range from −40°C to +125°C with an accuracy better than ±2°C and typically ±1°C at +25°C. Usefully, each of the sensors in the TMP35 series produces an output voltage that is linearly proportional to the Celsius (centigrade) temperature, as illustrated by Fig. 9.1. All three devices are available in low cost three-pin TO92 plastic packages.

The TMP35 series of sensors are intended for single-supply operation from 2.7 V to 5.5 V and this makes them eminently suitable for operation from the micro:bit's on-board +3.3V supply. To avoid the risks associated with self-heating the chip requires only a very small supply current (well below 50μA). In conjunction with the low supply voltage this ensures that the total internal power dissipation is less than 200μW.

The TMP35 temperature sensor provides an output of 250 mV at 25°C and is suitable for sensing temperatures in the range +10°C to +125°C. Other devices in the series are specified from −40°C to +125°C (TMP36) and +5°C to +100°C (TMP37).

The TMP36 temperature sensor produces an output voltage of 750 mV at +25°C whilst the TMP37 produces 500 mV at the same temperature (see Fig. 9.1).

To help you select the right sensor we've listed their characteristics in Table 9.1. For most applications and to indicate the widest range of temperatures, we would recommend the TMP36 sensor.

Interfacing TMP35 sensors to the micro:bit

The interface to one of the mictro:bit's analogue inputs is extremely simple and no other components are required apart from the temperature sensor itself.

Only three connections are needed; the +3.3V supply, the analogue output from the interface, and a ground (GND) connection. The pin connections for TMP35, TMP36 and TMP37 temperature sensors are shown in Fig. 9.3.

Characteristic	TMP35	TMP36	TMP37
Useful temperature range	+10°C to +125°C	-40°C to +125°C	+5°C to +100°C
Output voltage at 25°C	250mV	750mV	500mV
Temperature characteristic	10mV/°C	10mV/°C	20mV/°C

Table 9.1 TMP35 series specifications

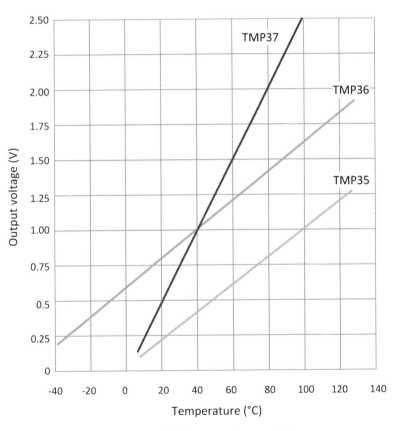

Figure 9.1 TMP35 series characteristics

Using the LM35 series of temperature sensors

The LM35 series of precision integrated-circuit temperature sensors provides another simple solution to temperature sensing with a micro:bit. Like the TMP35 series that we've just mentioned, the output voltage from the LM35 is linearly proportional to the centigrade temperature.

At normal room temperature, accuracies of around ±0.25°C can be achieved. Over the full −55°C to +150°C range the accuracy is around ±1°C (comparable with the TMP35 series). The LM35 thus offer somewhat higher accuracy than the TMP35 series at normal room temperature but, for many applications an accuracy of better than ±1°C is perfectly adequate.

The LM35 series of temperature sensors consume around 50 µA from a 3.3V supply and also exhibit very low self-heating (less than 0.1°C in still air). The LM35 is supplied in various packages including a plastic TO-92 package.

Interfacing LM35 sensors to the micro:bit

As with the TMP35 series, interfacing an LM35 temperature sensor to the micro:bit is extremely simple and, once again, only three connections are required; +3.3V, GND and analogue output.

The pin connections for the TO92 packaged version of the device are the same as those for the TMP35 (see Fig. 9.3).

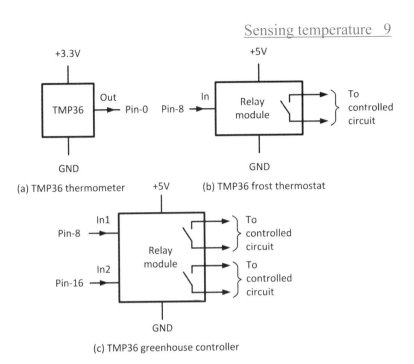

Figure 9.2 Circuit of the micro:bit thermometer/thermostat

Going further—a micro:bit thermometer and thermostat

To put all of this into context our eighth project involves the construction of a micro:bit digital thermometer and thermostat. Fig.9.2 shows how a TMP36 sensor can be very easily interfaced to the micro:bit. The two 100nF capacitors shown in Fig. 9.3 help to reduce noise which may be a problem in some environments, particularly where stray RF signals are present and when long connecting leads are used. The arrangement shown in Fig. 9.2 will provide indications over a temperature range

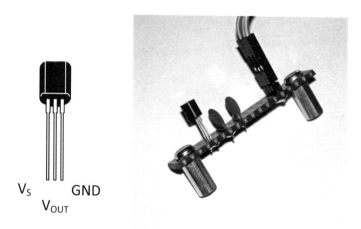

V_S GND
V_{OUT}

Figure 9.3 The temperature sensor is mounted on strip board

extending from −20°C to +100°C with an accuracy of around ±1°C. The analogue output voltage from the TMP36 is connected to pin-0 on the micro:bit.

The temperature sensor is mounted on a small piece of perforated strip board, as shown in Fig. 9.3. This board is linked to the micro:bit by means of flying leads or a short length of three-core cable.

The code for the micro:bit thermometer is shown in Fig. 9.6. Note that we've have used the powerful map code block (available from the Pins library) to convert the analogue voltage from the TMP36 sensor to provide an indication in centigrade. The map function saves a great deal of awkward calculation!

The basic thermometer project can be easily extended to increase its functionality. For example, a relay module can

Figure 9.4 The completed micro:bit thermometer

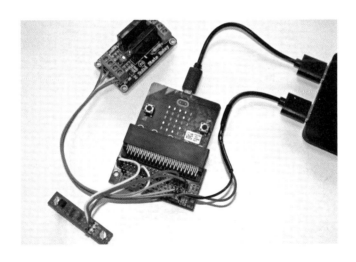

Figure 9.5 The micro:bit frost thermostat

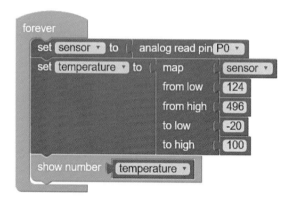

Figure 9.6 Code for the micro:bit thermometer

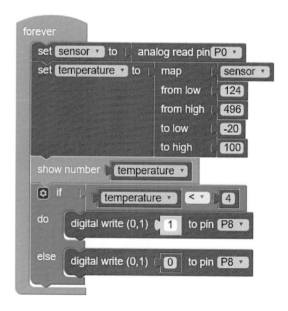

Figure 9.7 Code for the micro:bit frost thermostat

be added (see pages 62 to 64) so that the circuit will provide thermostatic control for a frost heater. The code shown in Fig. 9.7 takes pin-8 high in order to switch a relay module supplying power to a water pipe heater.

A further refinement is shown in Fig. 9.2(c) and it uses a two-channel relay module. The corresponding code

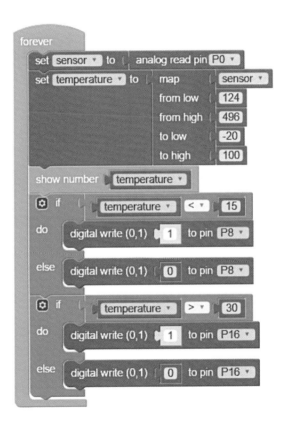

Figure 9.8 Code for the micro:bit greenhouse controller

appears in Fig. 9.8. The code is designed to maintain the temperature in a greenhouse within a fixed range (15°C to 30°C) and it provides two digital outputs (pin-8 and pin-16) and two pre-set temperature thresholds. Pin-8 will go high for temperatures below 15°C and pin-16 will go high for temperatures above 30°C. In the first case the relay will operate and supply power to a heater while in the second case relay will operate and supply power to open a vent or operate a fan.

Note that the code assumes that the relay module is activated when its input goes high. This was the case with the circuit described in Fig. 7.5 on page 63 but if the module is active low the code will need to have the 0 and 1 states interchanged in the digital write code blocks.

Questions

1. An analogue temperature sensor has a linear characteristic with an output that increases at the rate of 10mV/°C. If the output is 250mV at 0°C what will the temperature be when the output is 650mV?

2. Which of the three sensors shown in Fig. 9.1 is best for use at low temperatures?

3. The map function maps a variable from one range of values to another range of values. How are these range specified in a code block?

4. What typical accuracy can you expect from (a) a TMP35 sensor and (b) an LM35 sensor?

10

Sensing motion

Passive infra-red motion sensing

In conjunction with some form of alarm or lighting system, PIR motion sensing is an excellent application for a micro:bit. To further simplify matters, low-cost PIR sensors are widely available and they require minimal interfacing (just a +5V supply and a digital input on the microcontroller). Depending on positioning (see Fig. 10.1) a typical PIR motion sensor will be sufficient for a room size of about 16 m^2. This is ample for most domestic situations as well as smaller commercial properties.

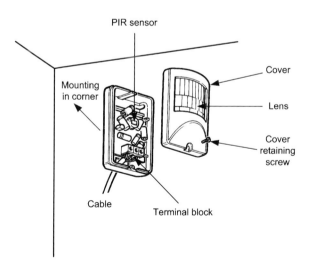

Figure 10.1 Typical mounting position for a PIR sensor

The PIR detection range depends on a number of factors, including the size and speed of the target object and its angular position relative to the sensor. It is therefore a little difficult to predict the exact range of any particular installation.

A typical low-cost PIR module is shown (with the PIR sensor chip exposed) in Fig. 10.2. In use, the sensor is covered with a lens (see Fig. 10.3). This not only helps to increase the angular response but also divides the coverage into sectors through which a target moves. The PIR sensor module can be connected to a micro:bit via an edge connector and one of the analogue input pins together with +5V and GND (see Fig. 10.5).

Before connecting a PIR sensor to your micro:bit it is worth testing the PIR sensor using a single LED, as shown in Fig. 10.5. The LED will become illuminated when the sensor has been triggered. You will then be able to make adjustments to assess working range and obtain optimum performance from the sensor.

Adjustments

After a moving target has been detected, the output from the PIR sensor module will go high for a period determined by the time adjustment pre-set control (see Fig. 10.4). This will hold the output high over a range extending from about 1 second (min.) to about 20 seconds (max.). Note that, when single trigger operation has been selected, there is a delay of about one second before the output changes from a low to a high. The remaining pre-set potentiometer provides sensitivity adjustment over a typical target range extending from about 1m to a maximum of about 5m.

Figure 10.2 The low-cost PIR sensor with lens cover removed

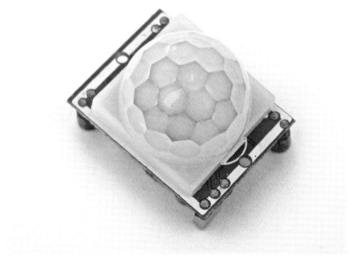

Figure 10.3 The low-cost PIR sensor with lens cover fitted

Trigger options

The low-cost PIR sensor may be configured for two different trigger modes. The desired mode can be selected by means of the link at the extreme left corner of the board shown in Fig. 10.4. The trigger mode can be set for either single triggering or for continuous retriggering. In the former (single trigger) mode the output from the PIR sensor will turn on and off as a target moves through its field of view. In the continuous retriggering mode, the output from the PIR sensor will continue to remain in the

Figure 10.4 Rear of the PIR sensor showing the trigger link (left) together with the sensitivity (centre-left) and time (centre-right) pre-set adjustments. The three pins at the rear are (left to right) ground, output and positive supply

high state for as long as motion is detected. In this mode the output from the sensor will remain high for as long as the target is within range *and is moving*.

Going further--a PIR motion alarm

Our final micro:bit project is a simple PIR motion alarm. The unit uses a low-cost PIR sensor together with a relay module in order to operate a sounder or security light.

The complete circuit of the micro:bit PIR motion alarm is shown in Fig. 10.5. We've included R1 and D1 so that the PIR can be tested (as mentioned earlier). The output from the PIR sensor is connected to pin-0 on the micro:bit. The output to the relay module is taken from pin-1.

You should find that the LED, D1, becomes illuminated and the relay operated when you pass your hand over the PIR module. Having confirmed that the PIR motion alarm is working, the next step is to install the PIR sensor in its final location. This will require an appropriate length of miniature three-core cable.

Connections from the micro:bit to the relay module can make use of the header pins (for input) and the miniature terminal blocks (for output).

When the alarm has been *set*, and the unit is ready to detect motion, an 'S' will appear on the micro:bit display. When motion is detected, and the alarm has been triggered, a 'T' will appear on the display. To *reset* the alarm you will need to press Button A on the micro:bit.

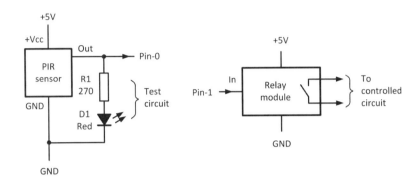

Figure 10.5 Circuit of the micro:bit PIR motion alarm

Figure 10.6 The completed PIR motion alarm on test

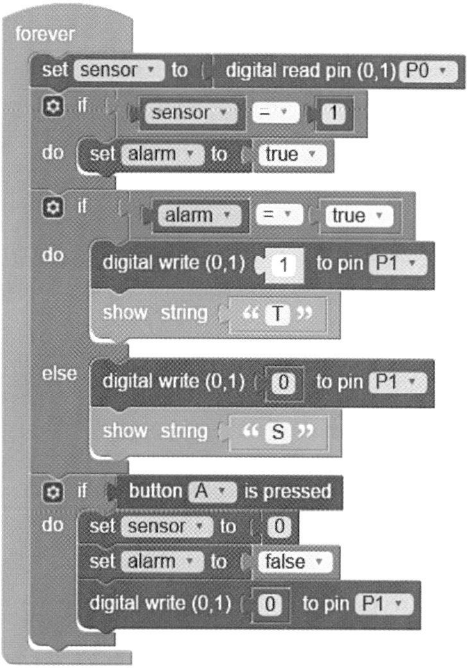

Figure 10.7 Code for the micro:bit PIR motion alarm

Some experimentation with the sensor's pre-set adjustments will normally be required but the adjustment procedure should be left until the PIR has been placed in position. With a little experimentation it should be possible to achieve the correct triggering, time and sensitivity. Note that, as with our last project, the code assumes that the relay module is activated when its input is taken high. If this is not the case the 0 and 1 states in the digital write code blocks will need to be interchanged (see Fig. 10.7).

Questions

1. What is the difference between the two trigger modes in which a PIR sensor module can be operated?

2. What is the purpose of the lens fitted to a PIR sensor?

3. What adjustments are normally provided on a PIR sensor module?

4. In the code shown in Fig. 10.7 what variable is used to represent the state of the output from the PIR module?

5. In the code shown in Fig. 10.7 what variable is used to 'remember' whether the alarm has been triggered?

6. In the code shown in Fig. 10.7, what three things happen when Button A is pressed?

Answers

Chapter 1, page 14

1. 25 individual LEDs in the matrix display plus one status LED on the reverse side of the board
2. Nordic nRF51822 32-bit ARM Cortex M0
3. 3.3V via the battery connector or 5V via the USB connector
4. Universal asynchronous receiver/transmitter
5. Via an edge connector (five of the larger pads also make can use of crocodile clips or 4mm banana plugs)
6. SPI (serial peripheral interface) and I^2C (inter-integrated circuit interface).

Chapter 2, page 24

1. A hexadecimal (.hex) file
2. The input library
3. By means of a drop-down list
4. Its value is increased by 1
5. It executes the code continuously until the power is switched off or is disconnected
6. 0

Chapter 3, page 34

1. Five rows and five columns
2. Bottom left: $x = 0$ and $y = 4$, top right: $x = 4$ and $y = 0$
3. The point function
4. To introduce a short delay for comfortable viewing
5. 256

6.   (1,3), (2,3) and (3,3).

Chapter 4, page 40

1.   To reset the processor and restart the program; on the rear of the printed circuit board
2.   Yes. By clicking on a small black circle shown below the image of the virtual micro:bit
3.   By placing a set brightness block inside a loop that increments the brightness parameter every time a button is pressed
4.   (a) To count up the change ... by parameter needs to be 1; (b) To count down the change ... by parameter needs to be -1
5.   (a) '?'; (b) '*'.

Chapter 5, page 48

1.   True (1) or false (0)
2.   Milliseconds (ms)
3.   Yes, provided the beginning and end of the inner loop is contained within the beginning and end of the outer loop
4.   count
5.   Displays numbers that count down each time Button A is pressed. The empty while ... do loop waits until Button A is pressed before continuing
6.   9 and 0.

Chapter 6, page 58

1.   (a) False, (b) False, (c) True, (d) True, (e) False, (f) True, (g) True, (h) True
2.   The else code block(s) are executed if the comparison evaluates to false

3. Yes, multiple else if blocks are possible
4. The code will display never display 'N' because the first comparison will always evaluate to False because the value of direction can't be greater than 315 and at the same time less than 45. This might apply to a compass bearing (in degrees) but it doesn't apply to ordinary numbers!

Chapter 7, page 72

1. 0V (or close) corresponds to logic 0 while +3V (or near) represents logic 1.
2. 5V is often used with small microcontrollers
3. Logic 1 (high)
4. Logic 0 (low)
5. (a) Pull-up resistor (to take the input high when the button isn't being pressed), (b) Pull-down resistor (to take the input low when the button isn't being pressed.

Chapter 8, page 84

1. Pin-0, pin-1 and pin-2
2. 10
3. 1024 (2^{10})
4. Approximately 0.032V (or 32mV)
5. analog read pin p0
6. No, the micro:bit uses pulse width modulation (PWM) and the analogue voltage produced is the mean value of this waveform
7. 682.

Chapter 9, page 94

1. 40°C

2.   TMP36
3.   The map function is used to map a range of values from one range to another range. The low and high values of each of the two ranges needs to be specified within the code block.
4.   Better than ±1°C

Chapter 10, page 102

1.   Single or continuous triggering.
2.   The lens increases the angular response and also divides the coverage into sectors through which the target moves.
3.   Output hold time adjustment; sensitivity adjustment
4.   sensor
5.   alarm
6.   The value of sensor is set to 0; alarm is set to false; the output from pin-1 is taken low.

Useful web addresses

Barclays	www.barclays.co.uk/bbc-micro-bit
BBC micro:bit Home	www.microbit.co.uk/
Kitronik	www.kitronik.co.uk
Mu	codewith.mu/
Samsung	www.samsung.com/uk/microbit/
Utronix	www.utronix.co.uk/
Element14	www.element14.com/
Jaycar Electronics	www.jaycarelectronics.co.uk/
Pimoroni	shop.pimoroni.com/
Rapid Electronics	www.rapidonline.co.uk/

Index

Index